Linguistics

H. G. Widdowson is Professor of
English for Speakers of Other Languages
at the University of London Institute of
Education, and Professor of Applied
Linguistics at the University of Essex.

Oxford Introductions to Language Study

Series Editor H.G. Widdowson

Linguistics

H.G. Widdowson

OXFORD UNIVERSITY PRESS

1996

Oxford University Press
Walton Street, Oxford OX2 6DP

Oxford New York
Athens Auckland Bangkok Bombay
Calcutta Cape Town Dar es Salaam Delhi
Florence Hong Kong Istanbul Karachi
Kuala Lumpur Madras Madrid Melbourne
Mexico City Nairobi Paris Singapore
Taipei Tokyo Toronto

and associated companies in
Berlin Ibadan

OXFORD and OXFORD ENGLISH
are trade marks of Oxford University Press

ISBN 0 19 437206 5

Set by Wyvern Typesetting, Bristol
Printed in Hong Kong

for b

Contents

Preface

Purpose

What justification might there be for a series of introductions to language study? After all, linguistics is already well served with introductory texts: expositions and explanations which are comprehensive and authoritative and excellent in their way. Generally speaking, however, their way is the essentially academic one of providing a detailed initiation into the discipline of linguistics, and they tend to be lengthy and technical: appropriately so, given their purpose. But they can be quite daunting to the novice. There is also a need for a more general and gradual introduction to language: transitional texts which will ease people into an understanding of complex ideas. This series of introductions is designed to serve this need.

Their purpose, therefore, is not to supplant but to support the more academically oriented introductions to linguistics: to prepare the conceptual ground. They are based on the belief that it is an advantage to have a broad map of the terrain sketched out before one considers its more specific features on a smaller scale, a general context in reference to which the detail makes sense. It is sometimes the case that students are introduced to detail without it being made clear what it is a detail *of*. Clearly, a general understanding of ideas is not sufficient: there needs to be closer scrutiny. But equally, close scrutiny can be myopic and meaningless unless it is related to the larger view. Indeed, it can be said that the precondition of more particular enquiry is an awareness of what, in general, the particulars are about. This series is designed to provide this large-scale view of different areas of language study. As such it can serve as a preliminary to (and precondition for) the more specific and specialized enquiry which students of linguistics are required to undertake.

But the series is not only intended to be helpful to such students. There are many people who take an interest in language without being academically engaged in linguistics *per se*. Such people may recognize the importance of understanding language for their own lines of enquiry, or for their own practical purposes, or quite simply for making them aware of something which figures so centrally in their everyday lives. If linguistics has revealing and relevant things to say about language, then this should presumably not be a privileged revelation, but one accessible to people other than linguists. These books have been so designed as to accommodate these broader interests too: they are meant to be introductions to language more generally as well as to linguistics as a discipline.

Design

The books in the series are all cut to the same basic pattern. There are four parts: Survey, Readings, References, and Glossary.

Survey

This is a summary overview of the main features of the area of language study concerned: its scope and principles of enquiry, its basic concerns and key concepts. These are expressed and explained in ways which are intended to make them as accessible as possible to people who have no prior knowledge or expertise in the subject. The Survey is written to be readable and is uncluttered by the customary scholarly references. In this sense, it is simple. But it is not simplistic. Lack of specialist expertise does not imply an inability to understand or evaluate ideas. Ignorance means lack of knowledge, not lack of intelligence. The Survey, therefore, is meant to be challenging. It draws a map of the subject area in such a way as to stimulate thought, and to invite a critical participation in the exploration of ideas. This kind of conceptual cartography has its dangers of course: the selection of what is significant, and the manner of its representation will not be to the liking of everybody, particularly not, perhaps, to some of those inside the discipline. But these surveys are written in the belief that there must be an alternative to a technical account on the one hand and an idiot's guide on the other if linguistics is to be made relevant to people in the wider world.

Readings

Some people will be content to read, and perhaps re-read, the summary Survey. Others will want to pursue the subject and so will use the Survey as the preliminary for more detailed study. The Readings provide the necessary transition. For here the reader is presented with texts extracted from the specialist literature. The purpose of these readings is quite different from the Survey. It is to get readers to focus on the specifics of what is said and how it is said in these source texts. Questions are provided to further this purpose: they are designed to direct attention to points in each text, how they compare across texts, and how they deal with the issues discussed in the survey. The idea is to give readers an initial familiarity with the more specialist idiom of the linguistics literature, where the issues might not be so readily accessible, and to encourage them into close critical reading.

References

One way of moving into more detailed study is through the Readings. Another is through the annotated References in the third section of each book. Here there is a selection of works (books and articles) for further reading. Accompanying comments indicate how these deal in more detail with the issues discussed in the different chapters of the Survey.

Glossary

Certain terms in the Survey appear in bold. These are terms used in a special or technical sense in the discipline. Their meanings are made clear in the discussion, but they are also explained in the Glossary at the end of each book. The Glossary is cross-referenced to the Survey, and therefore serves at the same time as an index. This enables readers to locate the term and what it signifies in the more general discussion, thereby, in effect, using the Survey as a summary work of reference.

Use

The series has been designed so as to be flexible in use. Each title is separate and self-contained, with only the basic format in common. The four sections of the format, as described here, can be drawn upon and combined in different ways, as required by the needs, or interests, of different readers. Some may be content with the Survey and the Glossary and may not want to follow up the suggested references. Some may not wish to venture into the Readings. Again, the Survey might be considered as appropriate preliminary reading for a course in applied linguistics or teacher education, and the Readings more appropriate for seminar discussion during the course. In short, the notion of an introduction will mean different things to different people, but in all cases the concern is to provide access to specialist knowledge and stimulate an awareness of its significance. This series as a whole has been designed to provide this access and promote this awareness in respect to different areas of language study.

H. G. WIDDOWSON

Author's Preface

It is, of course, impossible to do justice to the range and complexity of linguistics as a discipline within the compass of a small book like this one. And no such claim is being made. But it should be possible to identify the central issues it is concerned with and present a coherent outline of the area as a whole. This is what I have tried to do. And I have tried to do it in a way which makes ideas in linguistics clear without compromising their intrinsic complexity, which makes them more readily understood without diminishing their intellectual interest. This is not linguistics made simple but made accessible.

Of course, what counts as a central issue depends on how you identify linguistics as a discipline. Over recent years this has been a matter of considerable dispute, and there are those who would call for a radical revision of its scope and terms of reference, and would deny the validity of traditional principles of enquiry. In this book I have taken a relatively conservative line. This is not because I believe in conserving established principles of enquiry. On the contrary, I think their reappraisal is very much to be welcomed. But then one needs to know what they are. You can understand established ideas without accepting them, but it makes no sense to reject or revise them without understanding them.

It is a pleasure to acknowledge the contribution of colleagues and students over the years to my own understanding of linguistics, and the support I have received from Cristina Whitecross in writing this book. I have been greatly helped too by people who were kind enough to comment on earlier drafts: Nick Groom, Koo Yew Lie, Arthur Mettinger, Sonia Pokhodnia, Nahil Adel Uwaydah. I am most grateful to them. Anne Conybeare deserves a special mention: she subjected successive drafts to detailed critical analysis and pointed out all manner of defects and obscurities. Many, I am sure, remain, especially perhaps where I have stubbornly relied on my own judgement. But every book is inadequate in one way or another. And so it should be, for this then allows readers to get into the act, and piece out its imperfections with their thoughts.

My own imperfections are pieced out by the person to whom I owe the greatest debt, and to whom the book is dedicated. There is no more to say.

H.G.WIDDOWSON
Vienna, October 1995

Survey

Primacy of lg

1

The nature of language

Linguistics is the name given to the discipline which studies human language. Two questions come immediately to mind. Firstly, what *is* human language? How, in general terms, can it be characterized? Secondly, what does its study involve? What is it that defines linguistics as a discipline?

Clearly, the two questions cannot be kept completely separate. Whenever you decide to study anything, you have already to some degree defined it for your own intents and purposes. Nevertheless, there are a number of very general observations about the nature of language that can be made, and which will be the concern of this first chapter. These will then lead us into more specific issues in linguistics which will be taken up in subsequent chapters.

In the beginning ...

According to the Bible: 'In the beginning was the Word'. According to the Talmud: 'God created the world by a Word, instantaneously, without toil or pains'. Whatever more mystical meaning these pieces of scripture might have, they both point to the primacy of language in the way human beings conceive of the world.

Language certainly figures centrally in our lives. We discover our identity as individuals and social beings when we acquire it during childhood. It serves as a means of cognition and communication: it enables us to think for ourselves and to cooperate with other people in our community. It provides for present needs and future plans, and at the same time carries with it the impression of things past.

Language seems to be a feature of our essential humanity which enables us to rise above the condition of mere brutish beings, real or imagined. Shakespeare's Caliban in *The Tempest* 'gabbles like a thing most brutish' until Prospero teaches him language. In the play he is referred to as a monster, but that is better than being an ogre, who, according to W. H. Auden, is quite incapable of speech:

> The Ogre does what ogres can,
> Deeds quite impossible for Man,
> But one prize is beyond his reach,
> The Ogre cannot master speech.
> About a subjugated plain,
> Among its desperate and slain,
> The Ogre stalks with hands on hips,
> And drivel gushes from his lips.

We might note in passing, incidentally, that it is *speech* that the ogre cannot master. Whether this necessarily implies that *language* is also beyond his reach is another matter, for language does not depend on speech as the only physical medium for its expression. Auden may not imply such a distinction in these lines, but it is one which, as we shall see presently, it is important to recognize.

It has been suggested that language is so uniquely human, distinguishes us so clearly from ogres and other animals, that our species might be more appropriately named *homo loquens* than *homo sapiens*. But although language is clearly essential to humankind and has served to extend control over other parts of creation, it is not easy to specify what exactly makes it distinctive. If, indeed, it *is* distinctive. After all, other species communicate after a fashion, for they could not otherwise mate, propagate, and cooperate in their colonies.

The design of language

Other species communicate after a fashion. The question is after what fashion? Birds signal to each other by singing, bees by dancing, and these song and dance routines can be very elaborate. Are they language? One can argue that they are not in that they *are*

design features

indeed <u>routines</u>, <u>restricted repertoires</u> which are <u>produced as a</u> more or less automatic response, <u>and so *reactive* to particular</u> states of affairs. In this respect they <u>lack the essential flexibility of</u> <u>human language which enables</u> us to be *proactive*, <u>to create new</u> meanings and <u>shape our own reality unconstrained by the imme-</u> <u>diate context</u>. As Bertrand Russell once observed: 'No matter how eloquently a dog may bark, he cannot tell you that his parents were poor but honest'. <u>What are the features then (the</u> so-called **design features**) <u>which</u> provide for <u>such flexibility,</u> and which therefore might be said to be <u>distinctive of human</u> <u>language</u>?

<u>One of them is **arbitrariness**:</u> the forms of <u>linguistic signs bear no</u> <u>natural resemblance to their meaning</u>. The link between them is <u>a</u> <u>matter of convention</u>, and conventions <u>differ radically across lan-</u> guages. Thus, the English word 'dog' happens to denote a particu-lar four-footed domesticated creature, the same creature which is denoted in French by the completely different form *chien*. Neither form looks like a dog, or sounds like one. If it did, then dogs in France would be unrecognizable to English speakers, and vice versa. It is true that <u>some linguistic forms do seem to have a nat-</u> <u>ural basis</u>, that is to say, they are <u>in some degree onomatopoeic</u> (they s<u>ound like the thing they describe</u>). The word form 'bark' for instance, does seem, to English speakers at least, to sound like a dog. But it remains a <u>conventionalized link all</u> the same. The corresponding form in French (*aboyer*) is quite different. In German, the word is *bellen*: different again. And it is anyway hard to see what natural connection there might be between the English word for the noise a dog makes (no matter how eloquently) and the outer casing of the trunk of a tree.

We should notice, however, that although the link between form and meaning is arbitrary in this respect, that is <u>not to say</u> that <u>there is no relationship</u> between them at all. W<u>ords are arb-</u> <u>itrary in form, but they are not random in their use</u>. On the con-trary, <u>it is precisely because linguistic forms do not resemble what</u> <u>they signify that they can be used to encode what is significant by</u> <u>convention in different communities</u>. So the <u>fact that there is no</u> <u>natural connection</u> between the form of words and what they <u>mean makes it possible for different communities to use language</u> to <u>divide up reality in ways that suit them</u>. An example which is often cited is that of Bedouin Arabic, which has a number of terms for the animal which, in English, is usually encoded simply as 'camel'. These terms are convenient labels for differences important to the Arabs, but none of them actually *resembles* a camel. Similarly in English there is a whole host of terms for different kinds of dog: 'hound', 'mastiff', 'spaniel', 'terrier', 'poodle', and each will call up different images. But there is nothing in common in the different words themselves to indicate that they are all dogs. A 'spaniel' could just as well be a tool (cf. 'spanner') or a 'poodle' an item of oriental cuisine (cf. 'noodle'). And it is of course this very arbitrary, but conventional, connection between form and meaning which enables us to produce puns ('What's a Greek urn/earn?', 'My husband is a naval/navel surgeon', etc.). It is this too which can give rise to such amusement, or embarrassment, when we encounter words in another language which call up incongruous—often indelicate—associations because they resemble words in our own which have a very different meaning.

To say that linguistic signs are arbitrary in this sense is not to deny that they can be used in combination to onomatopoeic effect, that is to say where, to use Alexander Pope's words, 'the sound must seem an echo to the sense'. This is done most obviously, but by no means exclusively, in poetry, as in the line from Keats' 'Ode to a Nightingale':

The murmurous haunt of flies on summer eves.

Clearly, the language here is not arbitrarily chosen: it in some way *represents* the sound. But the effect can only be recognized if you know what the words mean: it does not arise simply from what they sound like. This is even true of the apparently onomatopoeic 'murmurous'. For if this word expresses a natural connection, with the sound alone evoking what it denotes, then why does the similar-sounding word 'murderous' not do so as well? It would seem to be the case in fact that it is only when you know the meaning that you infer that the form is appropriate.

A second design feature, one closely related to the first, is known as **duality**. Human language operates on two levels of structure. At one level are elements which have no meaning in themselves but which combine to form units at another level which do have meaning. In the line from Keats, for example, there is a repetition of sounds which are associated with the letter 's'. One of these sounds is voiced (the vocal cords vibrate) in the words 'flies' and 'eves', and the other unvoiced as in 'summer'. The same distinction corresponds to spelling differences in the case of 'v' (voiced, as in 'eves') and 'f' (unvoiced as in 'flies'). These distinctions are part of the sound system of English. But the sounds do not themselves have meaning. What they do is to combine in all manner of ways to form words which *are* meaningful. So although we can attribute no meaning to the sounds /s/ and /z/ or /f/ and /v/ as such, they serve to make up words which *are* different in meaning, as for example:

face /feɪs/   safe /seɪf/
phase /feɪz/   save /seɪv/

Obviously this duality provides language with enormous productive power: a relatively small number of elements at one level can enter into thousands of different combinations to form units of meaning at the other level.

So far we have considered duality in reference to spoken language but the same principle applies to written language as well. Here, letters enter into various combinations to form words whose different spelling signifies difference in meaning. As the examples given above indicate, sometimes there is a coincidence between sound elements and letter elements: the sound contrast in /seɪf/ and /seɪv/, for example, is marked by a corresponding spelling difference 'safe' and 'save'. But there are innumerable instances, and English is notorious in this respect, where the sound/spelling relationship is not at all straightforward (how do you pronounce the written word 'sow', how do you write the spoken word /saɪt/—'cite', 'sight', 'site'?) Languages differ widely in the degree and kind of correspondence between their sound and spelling systems.

The very fact that duality can operate with both spoken sounds and written letters in human language is itself a feature of its flexibility. No animal communication appears to have exploited other media to develop alternative delivery systems in this way.

It can be argued, and it usually is argued, that human language is primarily spoken, on the grounds that it is *originally* spoken, both in the individual's acquisition of a language and in the history of language itself. The written language is in both cases based on the spoken, and can be taken as a derived version. But we should note that each **medium** allows for a difference in **mode** of communication. When we talk of 'slurred speech' we refer to the medium; when we talk of 'a stirring speech', we refer to a mode, a way of using the medium to communicate in a certain way. Similarly, 'script' applies to the medium of writing, and 'scripture' to a written mode.

Once an alternative medium is exploited, different modes of communication emerge. Writing is delayed reaction communication. It does not depend on, and cannot exploit, a shared context of time and place: the first person addresser is at a remove from the second person addressee. In these circumstances, writing clearly allows for ways of talking about the world, and of communicating with other people, which are different from those which are characteristic of the face to face interaction of speech. In this respect, the development of writing from speech and its exploitation in various modes may be seen as further illustration of the inherent flexibility and creative potential of human language.

Animal communication

We may allow, then, that language is an impressive human achievement. But is it specifically and uniquely human? Is it **species-specific**?

One way of addressing this question is to compare the communication of other animals with human language to see whether it has the design features which we have been discussing. There is a difficulty here of knowing how to interpret the data as evidence. How many features, and in what measure of sophistication, does a particular type of communication have to have to qualify as humanlike in kind, even if not in degree? Animal communication may appear to us to be rudimentary, but we do not know how much of its potential is actually realized. It may be that birds and bees and dolphins could reveal more complex combinations of design features if the occasion were to arise. They may have more capability than their actual behaviour might suggest.

And anyway, it might be objected, how can we actually *know* the significance of the signs of other species since we can only interpret them with reference to our own? For all we know, the dog may be able to tell *other* dogs that his parents were poor but honest, in a kind of canine idiom we cannot understand. Our judgements are bound to be anthropocentric. We can imagine the possibility of linguistic sophistication among animals, of course. Children's fiction is full of talking animals. They figure in adult fiction too, often to satirical effect, as in Swift's *Gulliver's Travels* and Orwell's *Animal Farm*. But they are all anthropomorphic creatures, cast in our image; and using our language, not their own. The pigs in *Animal Farm*, for example, talk like human politicians. What their own distinctive animal idiom might have been, we have no way of knowing.

Another way of enquiring into whether language is species-specific or not is to try and get another species to learn it. The assumption here is that there might be some linguistic capability within animals which has simply not been activated by natural requirement. Perhaps the ogre only lacks appropriate instruction; perhaps his drivel is like Caliban's gabbling—evidence only of ignorance, not incapacity. Instead of just *observing* behaviour, therefore, what we need to do is *elicit* it, and actually try to get certain animals to learn aspects of human language. The argument is that if such animals can be induced to acquire language, it cannot in essence be specific to the human species. Since the non-human primates, especially the chimpanzees, are our closest evolutionary kin, they have been taken as the most suitable subjects for treatment.

It was recognized that these primates are not physiologically equipped with the kind of vocal organs suited to human speech, so that if they were to learn language it would have to be in dissociation from speech, through a different medium. Otherwise all you would get would be ogre-like drivel. One chimpanzee, Washoe, was brought up and instructed in the use of the American Sign Language (ASL). After four years she appeared to have a repertoire of some 80 signs or so, some of which she could use in combination. With another chimpanzee, Sarah, a quite different medium was used, namely a collection of plastic chips of different shape and colour, each of which was the token of a distinct meaning. To simulate human language, the relationship between the chips and their meaning was entirely arbitrary (a red square, for example, meant 'banana'). A more sophisticated version of the same sort of system was used with another chimpanzee, Lana, who was taught to press buttons on a computer installed in her room, each button having a different symbol inscribed upon it, again arbitrarily related to its meaning. Both Sarah and Lana learned a considerable repertoire of signs and were able to respond to, and manipulate a range of combinations suggesting that they might have acquired in rudimentary fashion some features of the flexibility so characteristic of human language.

The results of all these efforts with chimpanzees, however, have been unconvincing. Part of the reason for this is the disparity between the very efforts themselves and the relatively modest returns by way of learning. Human children appear to acquire language with impressive ease, and without the intensive and directed regime of instruction which the chimpanzees were subjected to. The fact that so much effort was needed to induce even rudimentary linguistic behaviour might itself be taken as indicative that the subjects lacked the capacity to learn. Certainly the chimps seemed somewhat lacking in natural language aptitude.

A related point is that whenever special conditions are set up as they were in these cases, with the use of chips and computer buttons, contrived contexts and constant monitoring, it is always possible that these conditions may have a distorting effect on the animals' behaviour. The chimpanzees may have been exhibiting an elaborate conditioned reflex rather than evidence of any more general capability. Human language provides abundant evidence that it is natural for humans to infer abstract categories from actual occurrences, to go beyond the immediate context, and indeed, as duality shows, to create a level of structure which is exclusively concerned with forms without meaning. It seems, judging from the evidence of these studies, that other primates do not have the same inclination to abstraction.

One reason for the human quest for abstraction of course, is that we are thereby enabled to categorize reality, and so in some degree at least to control it. As indicated earlier, language enables us to be proactive as well as reactive, and so, in some respects, to make the world conform to our will. It is interesting in this regard that the chimpanzees in question did not seek to use their newly acquired linguistic accomplishment with others of the species.

They appeared not to be aware of the advantage that language might bestow upon them. And this, of course, raises a very general (and obvious) question: if these animals, or any others, do indeed have a similar capacity for language as human beings, why have they never bothered to exploit it?

But this in turn raises another (equally obvious) question—and one which was touched on earlier. The researchers with Sarah and Lana recognized that the chimpanzees were physiologically unsuited to speech, so that if they were to learn language it would have to be through some other medium. But then not only are the conditions for learning unnatural, but what they are learning ceases to be natural language. This experimentation might well reveal interesting insights about the nature of chimpanzee intelligence, and this in turn might tell us something about what would for them constitute natural language. For all we know (at present at least) they might have a highly complex and subtle signalling system, a language comparable to ours, but exploiting visual and aural elements which do not count as significant to us. It would be interesting to know whether a latter day Tarzan would do any better among the apes than Washoe and Sarah among the humans. The attempt to teach apes human language reveals as much as anything else how incapable we are of conceiving of language in any except human terms.

Human language: endowment or accomplishment?

To return, then, to the question we started with: is language species-specific, unique to humans? The answer is that if 'language' is defined as '*human* language' and significance assigned to particular design features accordingly, then it is bound to be species-specific, by definition. But now another and more difficult issue arises. If language is uniquely human, does it mean that it is something we are born with, part of our genetic make-up, an innate endowment?

For it is of course quite possible to argue that something is peculiar to humankind and so is *generically* unique, without accepting that it is part of our biological make-up, that is to say, *genetically* unique. Thus, we might note that we seem to be the only creatures that take it into their heads to wear clothes or cook food, but no one, I imagine, is likely to argue that we are genetically predisposed to clothes or cooked food. It might be just as difficult to induce intelligent apes to adopt these human peculiarities on their own initiative as to get them to learn language. So it is hardly valid to use the linguistic shortcomings of Washoe and Sarah as evidence for the genetic uniqueness of human language. One might argue that their 'linguistic' behaviour is no more significant as evidence than the antics of chimpanzees at a circus dressed up for a tea-party. They can indeed ape human behaviour, but it is a travesty of the real thing.

So it is one thing to say that language is, as a matter of observable fact, a universal feature of the species not attested in other animals, and therefore a generic *accomplishment*; but it is quite a different thing to say that it is a genetic *endowment*. This is obviously a much stronger and more controversial claim. And it is one which informs the approach that the linguist Noam Chomsky takes to the study of language.

The argument for the genetic uniqueness of language is that it provides an explanation for a number of facts which would otherwise be inexplicable. One of these is the ease with which children learn their own language. They rapidly acquire a complex grammar which goes well beyond imitation of any utterances they might hear. They do not simply 'pick up' language, parrot-like, but use the language around them to develop rules which cannot possibly have been induced directly from the relatively meagre data they are exposed to. Acquisition is not, or at least not only, a matter of accumulation but also of *regulation*. So where does this capability for regulation come from? The argument is that it must have been there to begin with; that there must exist some kind of innate, genetically programmed **Language Acquisition Device (LAD)** which directs the process whereby children infer rules from the language data they are exposed to.

So the idea is that as human beings we are 'wired up' for language: that is to say for language in general, of course, not for any *particular* language. What (it is claimed) the LAD provides is a closed set of common principles of grammatical organization, or **Universal Grammar (UG)** which is then variously realized in different languages, depending on which one the child is actually exposed to in its environment. According to Chomsky, these principles define a number of general **parameters** of language which are given different **settings** by particular languages. The parameters are innate, predetermined, part of the genetic make-up of human beings. The settings are the result of varying environmental conditions. This being so, in respect to parameters, all languages are alike; in respect to settings, they are all different. In acquisition, children do not need to induce the particular rules of their own language from scratch, and only on the basis of the language data they hear. What they do is to use the data to set the parameters which they are already innately provided with. It is as if they came equipped for reception with all the wavelengths in place and all they need to do is tune in.

It should be noted that there is nothing especially novel about the idea that human beings are born with a cognitive learning capability which is wired genetically into the brain. What is different, and controversial, about this theory of innate universals is Chomsky's claim that we are equipped with a specifically linguistic programme which is unique to the species, and different in kind from any other capability. It follows from this view that language learning is not explicable as one among many aspects of general intellectual development, but only as the activation of a distinct language acquisition device and the growth of a kind of separate mental organ.

Language, mind, and social life

From the UG perspective, the essential nature of language is cognitive. It is seen as a psychological phenomenon: what is of primary interest is what the form of language reveals about the human mind. But this is not the only perspective, and not the only aspect of language, that warrants attention as being pre-eminently human. For although language may indeed be, in one sense, a kind of cognitive construct, it is not only that. It also, just as crucially one might claim, functions as a means of communication and social control. True, it is internalized in the mind as abstract knowledge, but in order for this to happen it must also be experienced in the external world as actual behaviour.

Another way of looking at language, therefore, would see it in terms of the social functions it serves. What is particularly striking about language from this point of view is the way it is fashioned as systems of signs to meet the elaborate cultural and communal needs of human societies. The focus of attention in this case is on what Michael Halliday calls 'language as social semiotic', that is to say, on language as a system of signs which are socially motivated or informed in that they have been developed to express social meanings.

The emphasis here is on language not as genetic endowment, but as generic accomplishment. There is little concern with the question as to whether human beings are absolutely unique in their use of systems of signs to express social meanings. It can be conceded that other animals use signs of various kinds to communicate with each other and to establish their communities. But the structure of these communities is simple in comparison with human ones and their signs are hardly comparable to the subtleties of the semiotic systems that have been developed in language to service the complex social organization and communicative requirements of human communal life.

With this social view of language, as with the cognitive one outlined earlier, there is a concern for explanation. Why is human language as it is? The answer this time, however, is that it has evolved not with the biological evolution of the species but with the socio-cultural evolution of human communities. Thus, one requirement of language is that it should provide the means for people to act upon their environment, for the first person (ego) to cope with the third person reality of events and entities 'out there', to classify and organize it and so bring it under control by a process of what we might call conceptual projection. In other words (Halliday's words) language has to have an **ideational function**. Another necessity is for language to provide a means for people to interact with each other, for the first person to cope with the second person, to establish a basis for cooperative action and social relations: so language needs to discharge an **interpersonal function** as well. And both of these functions, and perhaps others, will be reflected within the abstract systems of the linguistic code itself.

To the extent that these functions can be associated with systems of language in general, we may suggest that they too might be regarded as features of universal grammar (though not in the Chomsky sense). They will be realized differently in particular languages of course, but all languages can be said to plot their differences on the same set of general parameters. But in this case, these parameters are of a socio-cultural and not of a cognitive kind.

So language can be seen as distinctive because of its intricate association with the human mind and with human society. It is related to both cognition and communication, it is both abstract knowledge and actual behaviour. We can attempt to define its essential character by specifying a whole range of design features: its arbitrariness and duality, the fact that it is context–independent, operates across different media (speech and writing) and at different levels of organization (sounds, words, sentences), and *etc.* so on. The phenomenon as a whole is both pervasive and elusive. How then can it be pinned down and systematically studied?

This question moves us from the properties of language to the principles of the discipline which studies them, from the design features of language to the design features of linguistics.

2
The scope of linguistics

Experience and explanation

Language is so intricately and intimately bound up with human life, and is so familiar an experience, that its essential nature is not easy to discern. If you are in the middle of the wood all you can see is the trees: if you want to see the wood, you have to get out of it. The purpose of linguistics is to explain language, and explanation depends on some dissociation from the immediacy of experience.

There is nothing unusual about this of course. As we have seen, it is one of the critical design features of language itself that it is at a remove from the actual reality of things. Its signs are arbitrary, and can therefore provide for abstraction: they enable us to set up conceptual categories to define our own world. It is this which enables human beings to be proactive rather than reactive: language does not just reflect or record reality, but creates it. In this sense, it provides us with an explanation of experience. Of course, the languages of different communities will represent different variants of reality, so the explanation of experience is a matter of cultural custom and linguistic convention.

But this very ability to abstract from the actual—in other words, this process of thinking which seems to distinguish humans and their language from the communication of other animals—naturally sets limits on our apprehension of the external world. Our categories inevitably confine our understanding by defining it, and no matter how subtle they may be, they cannot capture everything. And they remain necessarily unstable. The abstracting, thinking process does not stop; we are forever calling our categories into question, adapting them to changing circumstances. We subject our reality to a continual process of conceptual realignment and look for alternative explanations. It is intrinsic to the nature of language that it allows for this endless adjustable abstraction, and the emergence of different ways of accounting for things. It contains within itself the dynamic potential for change.

The abstracting potential of language provides the means for intellectual enquiry, for the development of more formal explanation such as is practised in academic disciplines. We can think of such disciplines as cultures, ways of thinking and talking about things which are accepted as conventional within particular communities of scholars. As such, and as with any other culture, they draw abstractions from the actuality of experience. Linguistics is a discipline like any other. What is distinctive about it is that it uses the abstracting potential of language to categorize and explain language itself.

Models and maps

The experience of language, as cognition and communication, is, as we have seen, inordinately complex. The purpose of linguistics is to provide some explanation of this complexity by abstracting from it what seems to be of essential significance. Abstraction involves the idealization of actual data, as part of the process of constructing **models** of linguistic description. These models are necessarily at a remove from familiar reality and may indeed bear little resemblance to it. There is, again, nothing peculiar about linguistics in this regard. Other disciplines devise models of a similar sort. The way in which the discipline of physics models the physical world in terms of waves and particles bears no relationship to the way we experience it. This does not invalidate the model. On the contrary, its very validity lies precisely in the fact that it reveals what is *not* apparent.

The purpose of linguistics, then, is to provide models of language which reveal features which are not immediately apparent. That being so, they are necessarily an abstraction, at a remove from familiar experience. A model is an idealized version of reality: those features which are considered incidental are stripped away in order to give prominence to those features which are considered essential. In this respect, models can be likened to maps.

A map does not show things as they really are. No matter what its scale, a vast amount of detail is inevitably left out because there is no room for it. And even when there is room, details will be excluded to avoid clutter which might distract attention from what is considered essential. Consider, for example, the map of the London Underground:

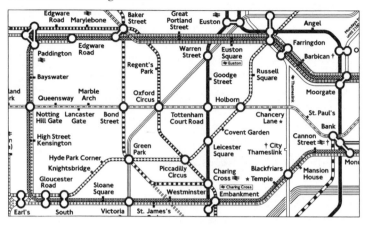

FIGURE 2.1 *London Underground map*

This bears very little resemblance to the actual layout of the track the trains run on, the twists and turns it takes as it threads its way underground. It gives no indication either about the distances between stations. It is even more remote from the reality of London above ground with its parks and public buildings and intricate network of streets. Such a map would be quite useless for finding your way on foot. It is in effect a model of the underground transport system designed as a guide to the traveller using it, and it leaves out everything which is not relevant to that purpose. It would be perverse to complain that it does not capture the full reality of the railway in all its complexity, misrepresents actual distances, and reveals nothing of what London is like at street level.

And so it is with models of the complex landscape of language. They will identify certain features as being of particular significance and give them prominence by avoiding the distraction of detail. Other features will be disregarded. And, naturally, different models will work to different scales and give preference to different features. Like maps, all models are simplified and selective. They are idealized versions of reality, designed to reveal certain things by concealing others. There can be no all-purpose model, any more than there can be an all-purpose map. Their validity is always relative, never absolute. They are designed to explain experience, and so they should not be expected to correspond with it. None of them can capture the truth, the whole truth, and nothing but the truth. If they did that, they would cease to be models, of course, just as a map which corresponded exactly to the terrain would cease to be a map. In both cartography and linguistics the problem is to know what scale to use, what dimensions to identify, and where, in the interests of explanation, to draw the line between idealized abstractions and actual particulars.

Dimensions of idealization

If we consider the actual particulars of language, they appear to be a bewildering assortment of different facets. As a means of interaction between people, language is a social phenomenon. It enables us to give public expression to private experience and so to communicate and commune with others, to arrive at agreed meanings and to regulate relationships. For this purpose to be served, different languages have to be relatively stable codes which people contract into as a condition of membership of the communities that use them, and there have to be generally agreed ways of using the language in different kinds of social context. In this sense, to learn a language is an act of social conformity.

At the same time, language provides the means for non-conformist self-expression as well. There is always some room for individual manoeuvre. For example, an individual speaking French, or Swahili, or Chinese in the natural course of events will on the one hand produce instances of that language, combinations of words, in accordance with the underlying systems of rules and established meanings which constitute the linguistic codes in each case. But on the other hand, they will be producing unique expressions in the language by exploiting the potential of the code. Although individuals are constrained by conventions of the code and its use, they exploit the potential differently on different occasions and for different purposes. But this conscious exploitation is not the only source of variation. The patterning of a person's use of language is as naturally distinctive as a fingerprint. And even spoken utterances repeated by the same person, though they may sound identical, are never acoustically alike in every particular. It is obviously socially necessary to assume that certain things are the same, even if, on closer scrutiny, they turn out to be different.

The point then is that, from one perspective, language is a very general and abstract phenomenon. It is a shared and stable body of knowledge of linguistic forms and their function which is established by convention in a community. At the same time, it is very particular and variable if we look at the actuality of linguistic behaviour. Since social control is necessarily a condition on individual creativity, there is no contradiction here. It is simply that the nearer you get to actuality along the scale of idealization, the more differences you discern as the more general abstractions disappear. It is therefore convenient to mark off limiting points along this scale to define the scope of linguistic enquiry.

Langue and *parole*

One such mark was made by Ferdinand de Saussure, the Swiss scholar usually credited with establishing the principles of modern linguistics. In a celebrated series of lectures in the early part of the century, he proposed that linguistics should concern itself with the shared social code, the abstract system, which he called **langue**, leaving aside the particular actualities of individual utterance, which he called **parole**. *Langue* was, on his account, a collective body of knowledge, a kind of common reference manual, copies of which were acquired by all members of a community of speakers. This distinction from language as actual speech can be justified on two grounds (and it is not always entirely clear which one Saussure is arguing for). Firstly, it is convenient in that it delimits an area of enquiry which is manageable: it is possible in principle to conceive of a linguistics of *parole*, but the individual particularities of actual acts of speech are so varied and heterogeneous as to be elusive of description. Secondly, the concept of *langue* can be said to capture the central and determining aspect of language itself. On this account, *parole* is the contingent executive side of things, the relatively superficial behavioural reflexes of knowledge. So *langue* can either be seen as a convenient principle of linguistics, or as an essential principle of language itself, or both.

There are a number of issues arising from Saussure's distinction. To begin with, one should note that the concept of *langue* eliminates from language its intrinsic instability. Language is necessarily, and essentially, dynamic. It is a process, not a state, and changes over time to accommodate the needs of its users. In fact Saussure was well aware of this. He was himself schooled in the tradition of historical linguistics which sought to account for changes in language over time, its **diachronic** dimension. But he conceives of *langue* as a cross-section of this process at a particular time, a **synchronic** state, which might be represented in the following diagram:

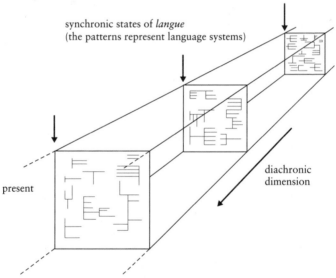

synchronic states of *langue*
(the patterns represent language systems)

diachronic
dimension

present

FIGURE 2.2 *The relationship between synchronic and diachronic aspects of language*

One difficulty about this conception, however, is that there is a confusion between synchrony and stability. Wherever you take a synchronic slice through language you will find not fixity, but flux. This is because language does not just change *over time* but varies *at any one time*, and indeed this cannot be otherwise because the members of a community which 'shares' a language will themselves be of different ages, will use language differently, and will have different communicative and communal uses for it. Different generations generate differences. No matter how small the period of time, or limited the variety of language, there will be variations within it as it is fine-tuned by the community of its users. And as some of these variable uses become conventionalized, so they become established as changed forms. In other words, diachronic change over time is simply, and inevitably, a result of synchronic variation at any one time.

To illustrate his synchrony–diachrony distinction, Saussure drew an analogy with the game of chess. The synchronic cross-section of language (the state of *langue*) is, he argued, like the state of play at one time. We can study the disposition of the pieces on the board without considering the diachronic dimension of the game, that is to say, the moves that were made beforehand, or those that might be planned in the future. We can, in other words, see the pattern of pieces as a state of play and disregard it as a stage in the game. The analogy breaks down, however, because of course the game of chess is of its nature a sequence of separate stages and the game itself stops as each player takes a turn. But language is a continuity with no divisions of this kind. It is linguistics which makes it stop.

To say that diachrony and synchrony are not in reality distinct dimensions is not to invalidate the idealization that makes them distinct, but only to set limits on its claims to absolute validity. And this, as has been pointed out, is true of *all* models of language. If we wished to account for variation and change, we would draw the lines of idealization differently, but there would still be idealization. And the resulting model would necessarily be less revealing of the relative stability of language which serves as the necessary frame of reference in accounting for variation. You have to assume fixed points somewhere as bearings on description.

And as bearings on behaviour. It is important to note too that this assumption of stability can have a reality of its own. It is not only Saussure who conceives of language as a stable state. Although a close scrutiny of an actually occurring language will reveal all manner of variation, people in the communities who speak it might well nevertheless *think* of their language as being settled and established, and accept the validity of grammars and dictionaries which record it as such. Members of a linguistic community may not have identical copies of *langue* in their heads, but they may nevertheless *believe* they do, and may consider whatever differences they do discern as matters of no real significance.

Competence and performance

A comparable distinction to that of Saussure, designed to idealize language data, and to define the scope of linguistic enquiry, is made by Noam Chomsky. He distinguishes **competence**, the knowledge that native speakers have of their language as a system of abstract formal relations, and **performance**, their actual behaviour. Although performance must clearly be projected from competence, and therefore be referable to it, it does not *correspond* to it in any direct way. As with other aspects of human life, we do not necessarily act upon what we know, quite simply because actions are inevitably caught up in particular circumstances which set constraints and conditions on what we do. So it is that actual linguistic behaviour is conditioned by all manner of factors other than a knowledge of language as such, and these factors are, according to Chomsky, incidental, and irrelevant to linguistic description. Performance is particular, variable, dependent on circumstances. It may offer evidence of competence, but it is *circumstantial* evidence and not to be relied on. Abstract concepts of competence and actual acts of performance are quite different phenomena and you cannot directly infer one from the other. What we know cannot be equated with what we do.

Chomsky's distinction obviously corresponds in some degree to that of Saussure. It represents a similar dichotomy of knowledge and behaviour and a similar demarcation of the scope of linguistic enquiry. There are, however, differences. To begin with, there is no ambivalence in Chomsky as to the status of the distinction. It is not that competence is presented as a *convenient* construct and therefore a useful principle for language study: it is presented as a *valid* construct, as the central principle of language itself. To focus on competence is to focus on what is essential and primary. Performance is the residual category of secondary phenomena, incidental, and peripheral.

A second point to be made is that though *langue* and competence can both be glossed in terms of abstract knowledge, the nature of knowledge is conceived of in very different ways. Saussure thinks of it as socially shared, common knowledge: his image is of *langue* as a book, printed in multiple copies and distributed throughout a community. It constitutes, therefore, a generality of highest common factors. But for Chomsky competence is not a social but a psychological phenomenon, not so much printed as *imprinted*, not a shared generality but a genetic endowment in each individual. Of course, individuals are not innately programmed to acquire competence in any particular language, but competence in any one language can nevertheless be taken as a variant in respect to universal features of language.

Langue, then, is conceived of as knowledge which is determined by membership of a social community, and so it follows that the focus of attention will naturally be on what makes each *langue* different. In this definition of linguistic knowledge, the main question of interest is: what is distinctive about particular *languages* as social phenomena? Competence, on the other hand, is conceived of as knowledge which is determined by membership of the human species and it follows that the interest here will naturally be not on what makes individual competences different but what makes them alike. In this definition of knowledge the main question of interest is: what is distinctive about *language* in general, and as specific to the human species?

Chomsky's distinction, then, leads to a definition of linguistics as principally concerned with the universals of the human mind. Indeed, he has defined linguistics as a branch of cognitive psychology. His idealization is a strictly **formalist** one in that it fixes on the forms of languages as evidence of these universals without regard to how these forms function in the business of communication and the conduct of social life in different communities. In this respect, Chomsky's definition of competence as the proper concern of linguistics is much further along the continuum of abstraction than is Saussure's definition of *langue*, in that it leaves social considerations out of account entirely.

Two further issues are perhaps worth noting in respect to this formalist definition of language. First, as was indicated earlier, it is obvious that the further one proceeds in abstraction, the greater the risk of losing contact with the actuality of language in use. If competence is knowledge of the abstract principles of linguistic organization, which may not be evident in actual behaviour, nor even accessible to consciousness, then what, one might reasonably ask, counts as empirical evidence for its existence? The answer to this question has generally been that linguists themselves, as representative native speakers of a language, can draw evidence from their own intuitions. But there seems no reason why one should suppose it as self-evident that linguists are reliable informants: on the contrary, one might more reasonably suppose that as interested parties with an analytic bent they would on the face of it be very untypical, and so be disqualified as representative speakers. There are ways of countering this argument, but problems about the link between abstraction and actuality remain, and the further language is removed from its natural surroundings, the greater the problem becomes. On the other hand, the more you locate it in its natural surroundings, the less you see in the way of significant generalization. The dilemma of idealization we discussed earlier will always be with us.

Whereas this first issue has to do with the methodology of linguistic enquiry, with how to give support to the statements you make, the second has to do with the scope of linguistic enquiry, with what your statements should actually be *about*.

And here we find something of an apparent paradox in Chomsky's position. What he represents as central in language is an abstract set of organizing principles which both define an area of human cognition, a specific language faculty, and determine the parameters of Universal Grammar. The various forms of different languages are of interest to the extent that they can be seen as alternative settings for these general parameters. The communicative functions such forms take on in actual contexts of use are of no interest at all. They furnish no reliable evidence of underlying cognitive principles: there are too many distractions in the data by way of performance variables. So the most important thing about language from this point of view is that it is evidence for something else, namely a faculty in the human mind, uniquely and innately specific to the species. In a sense, therefore, it would appear that what is central in language is that it is not of itself central. Paradoxically, for Chomsky, the study of language depends on disregarding most of it as irrelevant. Indeed, in this view, what linguistics is about is not really language but grammar, and more particularly that area of grammar which is concerned with the structural relations of sentence constituents, that is to say, with **syntax**.

Chomsky's specification of the scope of linguistics is extremely broad and far-reaching in respect to its implications, encompassing as it does nothing less than the universals of the human mind. But it is, of course, correspondingly extremely narrow and inward-looking in respect to the familiar phenomenon of language itself. What Chomsky presents is an abstract explanation of language which is a long way from actual experience. Not surprisingly, it has been challenged.

Knowledge and ability

One objection to Chomsky's model is that it defines the nature of linguistic knowledge too narrowly to mean a knowledge of grammatical form, and more specifically of syntax. Knowing a language, it is objected, involves more than knowing what form it takes: it involves knowing how it functions too. And this in turn implies knowing about words, not just as formal items, constituents of sentences, but as units of meaning which interact with syntax in complex ways. The formal systems of a language, after all, have evolved in association with words as the internal semantic encoding of some external social reality. So an account of grammatical knowledge, the argument runs, cannot ignore the fact that linguistic form is functionally motivated, so that to abstract form so completely from function is to misrepresent the nature of language. In this view, linguistics is essentially the study of how languages *mean*, how they are functionally informed: it is **semantics** which is primary.

Chomsky's *formal grammar* seeks to identify particular features of syntax with reference to universal and innate principles of human cognition. An alternative is to think in terms of a *functional grammar*, to consider how language is differentially influenced by the environment, how it is shaped by social use, and reflects the functions it has evolved to serve.

But it is also argued that knowing a language also includes knowing how to access grammar, and other formal features of language, to express meanings appropriate to the different contexts in which communication takes place. This too is a matter of function, but in a different sense. Here, we are concerned not with what the language means, that is to say, the *internal* function of forms in the language code, but with what people mean *by* the language, that is to say, what *external* function forms are used for in communication. Knowledge in the abstract has to be made actual and this is normally done by putting it to communicative use, not citing random sentences. People do not simply display what they know. They act upon it, and their actions are regulated by conventions of different kinds. So, according to this point of view, competence is not only knowledge in the abstract, but also ability to put knowledge to use according to convention.

There are then two ways of revising Chomsky's conception of competence, of redrawing the lines of idealization in devising a model of language. Firstly, we can redefine what constitutes the code or internal language by including aspects which reflect the nature of language as a communicative resource. This results in a functional grammar and, we may say, broadens the concept of linguistic *knowledge*.

Secondly, we might extend the notion of competence itself to include both *knowledge* and the *ability* to act upon it. Performance, then, becomes particular instances of behaviour which result from the exercise of ability and are not simply the reflexes of knowledge. Ability is the executive branch of competence, so to speak, and enables us to achieve meaning by putting our knowledge to work. If we did not have this accessing ability, it can be argued, the abstract structures of knowledge—this purely *linguistic* competence—would remain internalized in the mind and never see the light of day. We would spend all our lives buried in thought in a paralysis of cognition. Since this ability is only activated by some communicative purpose or other, we can reasonably call this more comprehensive concept **communicative competence**.

3

Principles and levels of analysis

However linguistic knowledge is defined, it involves an abstraction from actuality, some kind of classification of experience. To say that you know a language implies that you have *inferred* certain generalities from particulars. That is what we do in language learning. To say you know how to act upon your knowledge implies that you can reverse the process and identify instances, that is to say, *refer* particulars to generalities. That is what we do in language use.

Type and token

It follows that linguistic description deals in generalities, in abstract **types** of language element of which particular instances are actual **tokens**. Consider, for example, the following line from Shakespeare's *Richard II*:

I wasted time and now doth time waste me.

On one count, there are nine word elements here, and thirty-two letter elements. This is a count of token occurrences. But the word 'time' occurs twice, so if we count word types, there are eight words here. Similarly, if we count letter types, there are ten, since the letters 'i' and 'w' occur three times, 't' five times, and so on. But if we define elements differently, we would, of course, get other counts. Thus, we might count 'wasted' and 'waste' as tokens of the same type (the verb 'waste') or as different types if we are thinking in terms of **lexical items**, since the verb is used in two different meanings, 'to use extravagantly' and 'to make weaker and thinner'. Or we could adjust our focus again and consider vowels and consonants as different types of letter elements, and in this case we would have nineteen consonant and thirteen vowel tokens.

To identify an element as a token, then, is to recognize it as a particular and actual instance of a general and abstract type. But, as we have seen, we can distinguish types of very different kinds: vowel and consonant letters, word forms, lexical items, and so on. The question arises as to what the grounds are for distinguishing different types? In other words, what are the principles of classification in linguistics?

Principles of classification

Generally speaking, things are classified in linguistics in much the same way as they are classified everywhere else: on the basis of similarity. The philosopher Isaiah Berlin once made the observation that all philosophical enquiry developed from the formula: 'everything is like something: what is *this* like?' When we put two things in the same class we do so by identifying features they have in common and ignoring features which distinguish them. The question is, of course, *what* features do we take as significant? Take any number of things at random and you can always find some common features and therefore some criteria for classifying them as alike, no matter how different they might otherwise be. It is indeed of the very nature of language itself, as we have seen, that it enables us to impose an order on things in the physical world by classifying them in conventionally convenient ways. So the question is: what kind of likeness counts as significant in linguistic description?

It seems reasonable to suppose that it will be of a kind which is intrinsic to the nature of language itself. It was pointed out in Chapter 1 that one feature which appears to distinguish human language from the communication of other creatures is that of duality. This is the way the smallest elements of language, its sounds and letters, though meaningless in themselves, combine to form units at a higher level, i.e. words, which are meaningful. Since such combination of lower level elements to form units at a higher level is a defining feature of human language, one might assume that it would provide us with the principled basis for establishing likeness that we are looking for.

We can begin with examples cited earlier, in Chapter 1:

safe /seɪf/
save /seɪv/

The only difference between these words lies in the final consonant. In other respects they are a match.

The distinction between these consonants as sounds is that the first, /v/, is pronounced with a vibration of the vocal cords, that is to say, it is voiced; and the other, /f/, is not: it is unvoiced. Otherwise, they are alike: they are both produced by air friction between the teeth and lower lip and so can be classified as the same type of sound. But the point to be noted is that there is not only a **phonetic** difference between the consonants, that is they differ as physical sounds: there is a **phonemic** one too, that is their difference is functionally *significant* at the level of word formation. The two sounds appear in the same place in the spoken pattern /seɪ_/ and serve to produce words of different meaning. Similarly the letters 'f' and 'v' appear in the same written pattern 'sa_e' to distinguish the two words as written. So we can say that these consonants can be seen as alike, and put in the same class of elements, as letters or sounds, because they can both appear in the same place in the structure of word units. They share the same structural environment and have the same function of distinguishing words.

Other phonetic differences do not have such phonemic significance. Consider, for example, this pair of words:

pot /pɒt/
spot /spɒt/

The spelling of these words, and their representation as sounds, indicate that the sound /p/, like the letter 'p', is the same in each word: in other words, they are tokens of the same type. But the two /p/s are phonetically distinct. That in /pɒt/ is pronounced with a little puff of air, or aspiration, whereas that in /spɒt/ is not. This is not just a peculiarity of these two words but is a general feature of the sound patterns of English: whether the sound is aspirated or not is determined by what it combines with. When /p/ is stressed in word initial position, there will be aspiration, but not when it follows /s/. This means, of course, that, unlike /f/ and

/v/, aspirated and unaspirated /p/ cannot occur in the same structural environment. In other words, aspiration is a phonetic difference which is not phonemically significant in English.

But it may be, of course, in other languages. Different sound systems will make differential use of phonetic features. This, of course, creates problems when we encounter languages other than our own. We tend to associate phonetic differences with the phonemic distinctions we are familiar with. If, for example, the difference between /f/ and /v/ is not phonemically significant in a particular language, its speakers might well find the difference difficult to perceive, and would be likely to hear /seɪf/ and /seɪv/ as the same word.

The sounds of a language can then be classified by reference to their function in the duality of patterning, to the way they combine as constituents of words, which are higher level units. But this principle of classification is not confined to the duality relationship between sounds and words. It applies at all levels of linguistic description.

Dimensions of analysis

As is clear from the examples we have been considering, the classification of sounds is based on the possibility of their appearing in the same structural environment. This means that in classification we are concerned with two kinds of relationship. One of these is *sameness*: /f/ and /v/ each relate to the same environment /seɪ_/. The other is *difference*: /f/ and /v/ relate contrastively to each other *because* they appear in the same environment. As a further example, take the following words:

/pæt/
/pɪt/   /bæt/

We have here two minimal pairs, /pæt/ and /pɪt/; /pæt/ and /bæt/. What this means is that in the first case the vowels, /æ/ and /ɪ/, combine with the same surrounding consonants (/p_t/) and in the second case the consonants, /p/ and /b/, combine with the same sequence /_æt/.

When elements combine with others along a horizontal dimension, they enter into what is known as a **syntagmatic** relationship.

So /p/, /æ/, and /t/, for example, combine syntagmatically in the word /pæt/. But /ɪ/ can also appear in this environment to form /pɪt/ (and other vowels can as well, of course, to produce, for example, /pɒt/, and /pet/). Elements which have the same potential for appearance in the same environment in this way are said to be in **paradigmatic** relationship.

We can show these relationships in a simple diagram as follows:

```
p   æ   t
    ɪ
    ɒ
    e
```

Along the horizontal dimension, we have syntagmatic elements in *combination*. Along the vertical dimension we have paradigmatic elements in *association*.

And the same principle of classification applies when we consider other levels of description. Take, for example, 'pat' and 'pet', but considered now not as combinations of sound elements but as word units. They too can appear in the same environment when they combine into phrase units:

a pat	the friendly pat	that pat	that pat that stirred up all the trouble
pet	pet	pet	pet

The two words are paradigmatically associated in that they have the same possibility of combination in these structures. But the words do not, of course, have to be of similar phonological or graphological cut like these. Innumerable other word units of all shapes and sizes can also figure in such structures: ('patch', 'platitude', 'man', 'postman', 'face', 'embrace', 'approach', 'agreement', 'rivalry', 'mob', 'match', 'market', 'multitude'—and so on). Words which can enter into environments like these (a ..., the ..., that ..., etc.) are classified accordingly, as nouns. This is a very general class of words, of course, (one of the traditional parts of speech) and a closer look at possibilities of combination would enable us to refine the classification in various ways. All nouns, for example, can appear in the environment of a preceding article (the ..., a ...), but some, like 'pat' and 'pet', are normally required to appear in it, and others, like 'paternity' and 'petulance' are not so constrained. So in this respect 'pat' and 'pet' are in a different sub-class of words (count nouns) from 'paternity' and 'petulance' (which are non-count nouns).

The same principle applies to the combination of phrases in sentence units. Consider, for example:

The pat was offensive.

We can replace the first phrase here, 'The pat', with innumerable other phrases:

The friendly pat
~~The pat on the back~~
The pattern on the wall
The politician's speech
The pitter patter of tiny feet

All of these expressions, and infinitely many more, can all combine with '…was offensive'. So they all have the same syntagmatic relation with the rest of the sentence, they can all figure in the same place in its structure. Although they are all different in their own internal structure, they all have this equivalent function as a **constituent** in sentence structure. In this respect they can all be classed paradigmatically as noun phrases.

The forms of language, then, at any level, are organized along two dimensions or axes. They combine into larger structures along the horizontal or syntagmatic axis: sounds or letters combine to form words; words combine to form phrases; phrases combine to form sentences. When different forms have the same possibility of occurrence in a structure at a particular level, and are therefore equivalent in function, they are paradigmatically associated as members of the same class of items.

It is easy to see that this two-dimensional mode of organization provides the potential to generate infinite expressions from finite means and is the essential source of the creativity and flexibility which we identified earlier as distinctive design features of human language. These two interdependent dimensions accordingly represent the basic principles for all linguistic analysis at all levels. 'Everything is like something: what is *this* like?' In linguistics we can rephrase the question: 'Everything is paradigmatically associated with something when it fits into the same syntagmatic slot: what is *this* associated with?' The question always is: how do bits of language combine and how, therefore, can we associate different bits of language as functionally in the same class.

Levels of analysis

Given a piece of language, we can, obviously enough, describe it in different ways, at different levels of analysis. A word can be taken as a combination of letters or sounds, a constituent of a sentence, or an isolated unit of meaning like a dictionary entry. The analysis of language, as of anything else, can be adjusted to focus on different things, and this calls for a degree of detachment. With language, this is not always easy to achieve since our natural inclination is to engage with language and interpret it, rather than treat it as data to be analysed. Take, for example, this short passage of English:

WHERE TIME STANDS STILL
The history of Oxford is not a thing of the past. Here, time seems to hang as if judged guilty. In Oxford, people still ride bikes, wear gowns, have servants and live in gothic buildings.

Walking through the city, passing the crumbling walls of the colleges, it is easy to forget that it is the twentieth century... only the scaffolding gives it away. Apart from this intrusion, Oxford's air of the past remains undisturbed. This should not be altogether surprising since most of the colleges were founded well before the eighteenth century.
(*Oxford Handbook 1980–81*)

Here, we have an outdated description of Oxford which, for many, would be read as sentimentalized and distorted: not just outdated but outlandish. But reading and analysis are not the same thing. This is also language data, a sample of English which can be taken objectively as evidence of all manner of things depending on which level of analysis we choose to operate at.

So, we might, for instance, note certain facts about sound–spelling correspondences in English as exemplified here, in other words, the lack of congruence between its phonological and graphological systems. Thus, we have one **graphological** element 'i' which has two different **phonological** values (as in 'time (/taɪm/) seems to hang as if (/ɪf/)' and 'still ride' (/stɪl raɪd/) and three graphological elements, 'i', 'ui', and 'y', which have the same phonological value, as in 'if guilty (/ɪf gɪltɪ/)'.

We might, on the other hand, want to shift our attention to the level of words, and here we might note the way some of them are internally structured. We have quite a number, for example, which end in the letters *-ing*:

> th*ing*, build*ing*, walk*ing*, pass*ing*, crumbl*ing*, scaffold*ing*, surpris*ing*

We can point out that this sequence of letters '*-ing*', and the corresponding sequence of sounds /ɪŋ/, is actually a unit of meaning, but one which is dependent, which cannot occur on its own but only when attached to some word or other. And when it is attached it brings about various changes. So it can be attached to 'build', for example, and this changes the verb into a noun; or it can be attached to 'walk' and this makes it into a present participle. The '*-ing*' at the end of 'thing', however, does not have the same status, since there is no separate word *'th' in English that the unit can attach to. These observations are simple statements about the **morphology** of English words. And, of course, there are many other observations that might be made about these words at this morphological level of analysis.

Or we might wish to use the data differently and consider the words not as morphological structures but as vocabulary items signalling meanings of different kinds. That is to say, we might wish to focus attention on the words as **lexical items** or **lexemes**. We might note, for example, that in this passage, the association with Oxford keys us in to one particular meaning for the word 'gown' as specified in a dictionary and excludes others which might appear in the entry (like 'woman's dress, especially a long one for special occasions'). We might note the word 'bike' as an informal variant of the word 'bicycle'. We might contrast the occurrence of a common, ready-made formulaic sequence like 'time stands still', with the sequence 'time seems to hang as if judged guilty' which plays on an association of the words 'hang', 'judge', and 'guilty', and so breaks away from expectation (cf. 'time seems to hang heavily on their hands').

Consideration of the interdependencies and sequences of words leads us naturally into that level of analysis which is concerned with how they combine syntagmatically as constituents of larger structural units—phrases and sentences. Thus, we can treat this passage as a source of examples of English **syntax**. At this level, we might draw attention to the structurally equivalent sentences:

In Oxford, people still	ride bikes.
[In Oxford, people still]	wear gowns.
[In Oxford, people still]	have servants.

We can use these examples to discuss the difference between the overt *sequence* and the covert *structure* of sentences. Thus, part of the structure of the second and third sentences (shown in brackets) does not appear in the sequence at all. Or, again, the same structure can be manifested through different sequences. So we can have:

In Oxford, people ride bikes.
                        wear gowns.

Or the alternative sequence:

People ride bikes.
          wear gowns in Oxford.

In both sentences we have the same constituents in the same syntactic relationship: 'people' is the subject (S), 'bikes'/'gowns' the object (O) of the verb (V) 'ride'/'wear' and 'in Oxford', the adverbial adjunct (A). But this structure is manifested as the sequence ASVO in the first case, and as SVOA in the second. We might also wish to demonstrate cases where the same sequence signals different structure. Consider:

People, in Oxford, ride bikes.

Here we have the same structural relations between the constituents as before, but this time in the sequence SAVO. Compare this with the same sequence (with the commas removed):

People in Oxford ride bikes.

The phrase 'in Oxford' is now part of the noun phrase functioning as subject, i.e. 'People in Oxford', and has no separate status as a sentence constituent. The structure here, therefore, is SVO, without an adjunct A.

The question might then arise as to why syntax allows for these alternative sequences. This question takes us into another level of analysis. The fact that we can, at the level of the sentence, establish structural equivalencies underlying different sequences does not mean that these differences are insignificant. These expressions which we have been analysing as examples of sentences are here connected up in a **text**. As parts of a text, their function is to organize information in ways which the writer deems effective. So we might note that the ASVO version of the sentence has the effect of giving prominence to the place 'In Oxford', and since this is the topic of the passage which begins the first chapter of an *Oxford Handbook* this would seem to be appropriate. This sequence also patterns in with that of the preceding sentence, where there is similar fronting of the place adverbial:

Here, time seems to hang as if judged guilty.

This repeated pattern provides a kind of texture to the text, sets up a kind of connection or **cohesion** across the sentences. And the word 'Here' has a retrospective connection as well. We can only make sense of it if we relate it to the expression 'Oxford' in the preceding sentence. So we can point out a simple pattern in the text by tracing these cohesive links:

The history of Oxford is not a thing of the past. Here, time seems to hang as if judged guilty. In Oxford, people still ride bikes, wear gowns, have servants and live in gothic buildings.

But having embarked on an analysis of these data as a text, we might be drawn into other considerations. What kind of text is it? Of what genre? In a sense, this passage is historical since it is taken from the *Oxford Handbook 1980–81*. But who wrote it, and for whom? What purpose is it designed to serve? Whose reality does it represent, what kind of social attitudes, beliefs, and values does it reflect? To ask such questions is to go beyond the linguistic text to the social **context** to which it relates and seek to infer the communicative activity or **discourse** it records. So at this level, analysis approximates to interpretation and we ask not just what the text means in respect to its formal properties, but what the writer might mean *by* the text, and what the text might mean *to* a reader. We move into the domain of **pragmatics**.

At different levels of analysis, then, we focus attention on different features of language. We use the data as different kinds of evidence. Generally speaking, the larger the units we deal with, the less we idealize the data and the closer we get to the actuality of people's experience of language. But although it might be thought that our findings become thereby more valid, they also tend to get less reliable in consequence. On the whole, the more comprehensively we try to describe language, the more controversial the description becomes. In other words, a morphological analysis of word forms is relatively safe: pragmatic analysis of discourse meaning is relatively risky.

4

Areas of enquiry: focus on form

Different areas of enquiry within linguistics can be distinguished by the level of analysis which serves as their starting point. Thus, phoneticians start with sounds, lexicographers with words, grammarians with sentences. The next two chapters briefly sketch out the scope of these different areas of study, beginning here with those whose primary focus is on form.

The patterns of sound: phonetics and phonology

As was discussed in Chapter 2, language is both knowledge and behaviour. When we act upon our knowledge, we use some physical medium or channel (airwaves, marks on paper, electronic impulses, and so on) to produce perceptible behaviour in speech sounds or written letters. We make language manifest through pronunciation and spelling, that is to say, through spoken and written **utterance.**

But what makes the behaviour perceptible? When we listen or read, we do not process every physical feature of the utterance, but focus on what is significant. And in speech, as was pointed out in Chapter 3, significance attaches to those phonetic features which are phonologically distinctive, that is to say, which belong to classes of contrastive elements in the sound systems of particular languages. In other words, we filter out all kinds of phonetic differences and so perceive not the sounds as such but the **phonemes** they represent. The same principle of selective attention applies to written language as well. This is why handwriting can be legible in spite of individual quirks and oddities: we refer the variety of graphetic shapes to the underlying graphemic form.

The different *shapes* that sounds and letters take are perceived as tokens of the same type of *form*. With regard to speech, these variant tokens are called **allophones** of the same phoneme. It should be noted that on this account the phoneme is an entirely abstract entity: it can only be made actual through one of its allophonic manifestations. The same applies to writing. The **grapheme**, the written type, never actually appears on the page, but only some graphetic token of it. In both speech and writing, the tokens are elements of *behaviour* and types are elements of *knowledge*.

The study of allophonic manifestations, how the sounds of speech are actually made, is the business of **phonetics**. The study of phonemes and their relations in sound systems is the business of **phonology**. But these obviously have to be seen as intrinsically inter-related since the abstractions can only be *inferred from* the actual sounds, and the actual sounds as sounds of speech (as distinct from just vocal noise like coughing and snoring) have to be *referred to* the abstractions they manifest.

Sound segments

The term 'the sounds of speech' covers a range of phenomena. It can refer, for example, to separate segments: vowels and consonants. It is the concern of phonetics to describe how the vocal organs are used to articulate them and the concern of phonology to establish the conditions of their occurrence in relation to each other. A phonological account, while acknowledging the general validity of the physical description, will also point out that there is another factor which determines the identification of a sound segment, namely its distribution, or the range of positions in which it can appear in a word. As we have already noted in Chapter 3, for example, when the consonant /p/ begins a word, it is pronounced with a little puff of air, that is to say, it is aspirated. However, when it follows the unvoiced sibilant /s/, as in /spɒt/, there is no aspiration. This is a phonetic fact about the different ways this sound is pronounced in these different positions. But the differences are not significant in that they do not serve to distinguish one word from another. So there is no reason to make a phonological distinction: hence these aspirated and unaspirated sounds count as allophonic variants of the same phoneme, /p/.

Syllables

But the description of speech does not stop here, of course, for speech does not just consist of a string of separate vowels and consonants. These sounds are organized into larger segments called **syllables**. /pɪt/, for example, consists of one syllable (Consonant Vowel Consonant, or CVC), so does /spɪt/ (CCVC), and /splɪt/ (CCCVC), whereas /'spɪrɪt/ consists of two (CCV–CVC), /'spɪrɪtɪd/ three (CCV–CV–CVC), and /dɪ'spɪrɪtɪd/ four (CV–CCV–CV–CVC). Although a syllable (normally) has to have a vowel (and sometimes consists only of a vowel, as in the word 'eye' or 'I' /aɪ/ (V)) it can, as we can see, combine with several initial and/or final consonant clusters. But there are restrictions on the distribution of consonants in these clusters. These restrictions differ from language to language, and from dialect to dialect, and serve as criteria for establishing the phonological status of different consonant sounds. To take /p/ again, this, in English, can occur in syllable final position after /m/ (as in /læmp/); but /b/, in most accents of English, does not (as shown by the fact that the word written 'lamb' is pronounced /læm/ not */læmb/). This provides a phonological reason for distinguishing between the two consonants. In English again, it is common to find syllables with three initial consonants, but only on condition that the first is the unvoiced sibilant /s/ as in /strɪŋ/, /stretʃ/, /sprɪŋ/, and so on. And /s/ cannot occur in second place in an initial cluster, so we can have /spaɪk/ ('spike') but not */'psaɪkɪ/ (in the pronunciation of the corresponding written word 'psyche', the first letter is ignored). The same point can be made about written words like 'knot' and 'knowledge': English does not allow a syllable-initial cluster* /kn/. Other languages do. Actually the sequence occurs in English as well, but only across a syllable boundary, as in /'laɪknɪs/ ('likeness'CVC–CVC).

Stress and intonation

When a word has more than one syllable, one of them will be pronounced with more prominence than the others. This brings us to another speech sound phenomenon, that of **stress**. This may be a fixed feature of a word, and essentially part of its form, so that there is no real option in its placement. In English, for example, the nouns 'parson', 'witness', and 'wedding' will always be stressed on the first syllable, and the verbs 'inspire', 'provoke', and 'decide' will always be stressed on the second. It is worth noticing that it seems to be a general tendency in English to mark the difference between these word classes in this way: nouns have first syllable stress, verbs second. Sometimes this change of stress marks the class difference between words which are semantically similar, as in 'REcord' (Noun, or N) and 'reCORD' (Verb, or Vb), or semantically different as in 'REfuse' (N) and 'reFUSE' (Vb), or 'OBject' (N) and 'obJECT' (Vb).

In these cases, stress is a property of the words themselves. But stress can also be differentially applied by speakers to provide prominence to certain parts of what they are saying. Consider, for example, the following utterance:

The chairman may resign.

The words 'chairman' and 'resign' carry their normal stress patterns with them, but there is also a general tendency in English to give extra prominence to the last stressed syllable in an utterance, so the normal way of saying this (the unmarked remark, so to speak) would be:

The cháirman may resígn.

But I can choose to say this differently by altering the stress pattern, as in:

The cháirman may resign. (But nobody else will.)

The cháirman máy resígn. (But, then again, he may not.)

So stress is a feature of speech which ranges beyond the individual sound segments and operates **suprasegmentally** over utterances. And this is not the only suprasegmental feature. When producing utterances, our voice goes up and down, and plays a rhythmic tune. In other (more technical) words, we vary not only stress but **pitch** also. This patterning of stress and pitch gives a particular **intonation** to what we say. So it is that in reference to the remark about the chairman, I may change pitch and use a falling tone on the last syllable and so give it the force of a statement:

The chairman may resign.

Or I may give the last syllable a rising tone, and thereby give my utterance the force of a question:

The chairman may resign?

Or I might choose to use a rising tone to the stressed syllable in the marked version of the utterance. In this case the force of the question focuses on the chairman:

The chairman may resign? (Why the chairman?)

We can see from all this that although phonetics and phonology begin at the level of individual sound segments, they are drawn into a consideration of larger units like syllables, words and combinations of words, and eventually to the various ways in which we use stress and pitch patterns to express subtleties of meaning in utterances. In acts of speech, people use their voice as a complex instrument and, using the notes provided by the sound systems of their languages, produce infinite variations of meaning. Phonetics and phonology seek to explain how they do it.

The construction of words: morphology

A convenient starting point for **morphology** is the word. The word has already made its appearance in the previous section, where its structure was defined in terms of syllables. But it can be defined in other terms as well. The word 'parson', for example, has two syllables. So has the word 'parting'. In syllabic structure they are alike. But we can divide up the second word in another way as well. There is an independent lexical item 'part' in English and, as we noted in Chapter 3, '–*ing*' can be attached to the end of innumerable other words—'pars^*ing*', 'pass^*ing*', 'depart^*ing*', 'depress^*ing*', to give just a few examples. So we might propose that the word is made up of two elements of meaning, or **morphemes**, *part* and –*ing* the first of which is independent, or **free**, and the second dependent, or **bound**.

We might consider dismantling 'parson' in the same way. There are, after all, words which start with the same sequence of letters *par*: 'parcel', 'parking', 'parting', 'particle', and so on. But 'par' does not signal anything semantically in common, and *–cel*, *–king*, *–ting*, and *–ticle* do not seem to attach themselves as bound morphemes to any other words in English. We might try another division of the word and propose the morphological structure pars^*on* thereby involving an analogy with words like 'parsimony', 'parsley', and 'parsnip', but we would be no better off, since we cannot assign *pars–*, *–imony*, *–ley*, or *–nip* any morphemic status either.

It seems clear, then, that the syllable as a unit of sound has, in English at any rate, no correspondence with the morpheme as a unit of meaning. 'Parson' has two syllables, but consists of only one morpheme. 'Parting' has two syllables, and two morphemes.

Derivation and inflection

But things are not, of course, quite so simple. There is a further complication. 'Parson' is unambiguously a noun. 'Parting' can also be a noun, as in the phrase 'the parting of the ways'. But it can equally be the present participle of the verb, as in an expression like 'they were parting company for good'. In the first case, the attachment of *–ing* has the permanent effect of changing the word, of creating a different lexical item by deriving a noun from a verb. In the second case, the effect is temporary in that it changes the *form* of the word: here *–ing* alters the verb, or inflects it, to signal continuous aspect.

As this example indicates, morphology is concerned with two quite different phenomena: **derivation** and **inflection**. Derivation has to do with the way morphemes get attached as **affixes** to existing lexical forms or stems in the process of word formation. Some affixes, for example, *de–*, *dis–*, *un–*, and *pre–*, are attached at the beginning (i.e. are **prefixes**), and some (for example, *–ure*, *–age*, *–ing*, *–ize*, *–ful*, and *–able*) are attached at the end (i.e. are **suffixes**). So, for example, if we take the lexical item 'like' (the verb) we can add a prefix to this base or root form and make another verb '*dis*^like'. Or we can add a suffix and make the adjective 'like^*able*'. Add a prefix to this stem and we get '*un*^likeable'. Add another suffix and we get 'unlikeable^*ness*'. Or we can take the root 'like' as an adjective. If we add a prefix we get another adjective '*un*^like', add a suffix and we get a noun 'like^*ness*', add the suffix –*ly* to the root and the adjective gets converted into the adverb 'like^*ly*', add another suffix to *this* stem, and we get the noun 'likeli^*hood*', add a prefix '*un*^likelihood', and so on.

This immensely productive process of morphological derivation follows the same principle of creativity by variable combination which was discussed in Chapter 3 and which, as we have seen in this chapter, defines phonological processes. This, of course, is a distinctive design feature of human language. The difference is that in phonology the process provides for the generation of word forms as combinations of sounds, whereas in derivational morphology the process accounts for the generation of lexical items as combinations of meanings.

Inflectional morphology is different again. This does not create new words but adapts existing words so that they operate effectively in sentences. It is not a process of *lexical innovation* but of *grammatical adaptation*. Take, for example, the four lexically different verbs 'part', 'partition', 'depart', and 'departmentalize'. As verbs, their function is, by definition, dependent on the grammatical categories of tense and aspect, and this dependency is marked by morphological inflection, which is added on to any derivational morpheme there might be. Thus, for them to function in the simple past tense, the past tense morpheme is required ('part^*ed*', 'partition^*ed*', 'depart^*ed*', and 'departmentaliz^*ed*'). Equally, if they are to function in the simple present, a present tense morpheme is required.

The morphological marking for grammatical function also applies in English to nouns and pronouns, and in other languages to other word classes as well. Thus, 'departure', as a count noun, is subject to marking for singular and plural: 'a departure'/ 'several departures'.

Notice that, like the phoneme, the inflexional morpheme is an abstraction which is realized in various ways. It follows that just as we need the concept of the allophone, so we need the concept of the **allomorph**. Thus, there are a number of allomorphic variants, for example, for the past tense morpheme. It can be realized phonologically by /ɪd/ (graphologically 'ed') as in 'part^*ed*', or this graphological allomorph can be phonologically realized as

/d/ 'pull^*ed*' or /t/ 'push^*ed*'. Or the morpheme may be allo-morphically realized by more radical changes to the sound and spelling of the stem form as in 'sleep'—'sle*pt*', 'shake'—'sh*oo*k', and so on.

It is worth noting that these cases again illustrate the lack of correspondence between syllable and morpheme. In English there are many cases, like those already noted, where an inflectional morpheme does not figure as a separate syllable. And there are many other languages where a single syllable can incorporate several different inflectional morphemes.

Morphology, then, is the study of two aspects of words: their derivational formation and their inflectional function. The first aspect quite naturally leads us to enquire further into the way words mean, into lexical semantics, and this will be the focus of attention in Chapter 5. The second aspect leads us into a consideration of the way words function in syntax, and it is to this that we now turn in this chapter.

The combination of words: syntax

The inflectional attachments we have been talking about can be seen as coupling devices which allow words to function as constituents in larger structural units like phrases and sentences. This constituent structure is called **syntax**. Whereas morphology deals with the way words are adapted, syntax deals with the way they are combined in sentences. The two areas are obviously interdependent, and together they constitute the study of **grammar**.

To see how they work together, consider first a sequence of word stems, unadorned with any morphological inflection:

church gothic in live artist

If we wanted to make sense of this collection of words, we would come up with a different word order—one which in some rough and ready way indicated a possible state of affairs. For example:

artist live in gothic church

One thing that allows us to order the words in this way is our recognition of what kind of words they are. Thus, we identify 'artist' and 'church' as nouns and so potentially subject or object.

'Gothic' looks like an adjective (cf. 'rustic', 'realistic', 'fantastic') and so has to precede a noun, and 'church', rather than 'artist' seems the more likely candidate. 'Live' is a little more tricky since we cannot tell from its spelling whether it is a verb (/lɪv/, as in 'artists live') or an adjective (/laɪv/, as in 'live artists'), but since there is no other verb-like word in sight, let us suppose that it is the former. And so we come up with the semblance of a proposition, partially focused by the word order, but only partially. We have an indication that an artist (or more than one) is (or was) somehow involved in the process of living in one (or more than one) gothic church: but it is all rather vague and indeterminate.

Grammatical systems

This is where inflection comes in, of course. It can, to begin with, locate the event in time, setting the co-ordinates of past and present by marking the verb for tense. At the same time it marks the verb for aspect, that is to say, it represents the process as taking place either over an open period of time (progressive), or within a closed period of time (perfective), or left unspecified (simple).

Tense and aspect are systems which provide the verb with its formal identity as a sentence constituent. So if 'live' is to function as a verb, it has to be processed through the system and marked as such. Let us then select present tense and simple aspect. We now have a slightly more focused proposition:

artist lives in gothic church

Again, this might be sufficient to signal meaning. It might, for example, figure quite plausibly as a newspaper headline. But notice that our choice of inflection does not only signal tense and aspect, but singular as well, and as such it transfers the signal to the preceding subject. We specify one artist. But this needs to be formally marked as well (even though in certain uses, like headlines and telegrams, convention allows us to waive the requirement in the interests of brevity). Nouns also have systems which provide them with identity conditions. Just as verbs have to be processed through the dual tense/aspect system, so nouns have to be processed through the dual number/definiteness system. Are we talking about a single artist or artists in the plural, the artist or artists we know about, any old artist or an artist or artists unknown? We have to decide, and mark the noun accordingly; and the same, of course, applies to the noun 'church'.

If we then process our sequence of words through the required grammatical systems, we come up with a number of possibilities:

The artist lives in a gothic church.
An artist lived in a gothic church.
The artist was living in a gothic church.
Artists live in gothic churches.
Artists have lived in gothic churches.

And so on, and so on.

Constituent structure

Now there are a number of points that are worth noting here. Firstly, the processing of nouns and verbs through their systems has to be co-ordinated. The marking of plurality on the noun, for example, has to match up with a corresponding marking on the verb to which it relates. In other words, they have to fit together as interdependent constituents of a larger structure, that of the sentence.

Secondly, this preparation for constituent status may involve only the use of an inflection as in 'artists', 'lives', and so on. But it may also involve the deployment of separate morphemes, the so-called 'function words'. This is the case with English, for example, where such function words are required for the marking of definiteness, as in phrases like '*a/the* artist', '*is/was* living' and so on. So we can say that the noun phrases (for example, 'the artist'), and verb phrases (for example, 'was living') are constituents of larger structures, but are themselves in turn structured into constituents. Thus, the noun phrase consists of a noun as headword, and markers for number and definiteness. These markers too are interdependent. If you combine plural with definite, you need a preceding article '*the* artists'; if you combine it with the indefinite, you get only the inflectional form 'artist*s*'. Similarly, the verb phrase may consist of an inflected form on its own, 'liv*es*', or with various attendant auxiliaries '*is* liv*ing*' '*has* liv*ed*', and so on.

So far we have only been considering phrases of a simple two-place structure realized as article–noun (Art–N) and auxiliary–verb (Aux–V). It is easy to see that things can get much more complicated. Articles are not the only class of words which can figure at the beginning of a noun phrase, for example. We can also have demonstratives ('this', 'that', 'these', 'those') and possessives ('his', 'her', 'its', 'their'). Articles, demonstratives, and possessives are all classified as determiners and are part of a complex system. In general, phrases can be said to have the constituent structure Det–N.

But , as we can see from our example, we can also have a class of words intervening between Det and N, namely adjectives—Det–Adj–N ('the *gothic* church'). But adjectives have to be put in their place as well. If, for example, we wanted to add 'old' and 'derelict' to the words we started with, we can only do so in conformity with a certain conventional order: 'the derelict old gothic church' would count as normal and unmarked, but *'the gothic old derelict church' would not.

The order is not arbitrary. The proximity of the adjective to the headword—the noun itself in the noun phrase—corresponds with the closeness of conceptual association, or degrees of classification: 'the old gothic church' is an instance of a class of churches, i.e. gothic ones, which happens, incidentally, to be old; 'the derelict old gothic church' is one of a class of old gothic churches which happens to be derelict. It would be unusual to conceive of a class of derelict churches which were gothic (as distinct, say, from baroque).

Though this observation may seem a matter of trivial detail, the point it illustrates is a crucial one. As was noted earlier, the structural properties of language can be analysed in formal terms. We can talk about syntactic constraints which require words to be inflectionally modified in certain ways so that they can couple up correctly in combination. We can talk about the necessary or normal ordering of constituents in words, phrases, and sentences. But all this grammatical treatment has a communicative point. What it does is to adapt words morphologically and organize them syntactically so that they are more capable of encoding the reality that people want to express. There are times when grammar can be dispensed with because the context of shared knowledge and experience is such that only the simplest forms are necessary—'Hungry?'; 'Door!'. What grammar provides is the means to focus more precisely on relevant aspects of this context,

'Would you like to have your lunch now?'; 'You have left my door open, and I would like you to close it.' In other words, the formal properties of language are functionally motivated.

Within the noun phrase, then, there are tight structural constraints on sequence. The noun phrase itself, as a higher level constituent, is allowed more room for manoeuvre. We saw this earlier (in Chapter 3) when we noted the different ordering of constituents in the sentence: 'People ride bikes in Oxford'/'In Oxford, people ride bikes'/'People, in Oxford, ride bikes.'

But just as the tightness of control within the noun phrase is motivated, so is this relaxation of control of constituents within the sentence. Generally speaking, the larger the constituent, the greater its mobility. In all cases, the syntax provides a means to exploit more fully the meanings that are encoded in words.

The principles of constituent structure, based as they are on the syntagmatic and paradigmatic relations discussed earlier (in Chapter 3) are very powerful. They can produce (or generate) elaborate combinations and permutations of all kinds. Linguists will often demonstrate this by the invention of sentences of curious and baffling complexity, sentences which bear little resemblance to what people actually produce as utterances in real life. We have to bear in mind, however, that these sentences are devices for illustrating the syntactic means which speakers of a language have at their disposal, not the ways in which they actually employ them in contexts of use.

The morphological and syntactic processes which have been briefly outlined can be described in purely formal terms as operations of the code. But it is important to recognize that they function as devices for extending word meanings, and so constitute a communicative resource.

5

Areas of enquiry: focus on meaning

Meaning in language: semantics

The study of how meaning is encoded in a language is the central business of semantics, and it is generally assumed that its main concern is with the meanings of words as lexical items. But we should note that it is not *only* concerned with words as such. As we have seen, meaning also figures at levels of language below the word and above it. Morphemes are meaningful, for example: the derivational prefix *pre–* means 'before', so a '*pre*^fix' means 'something fixed before'. '*Un*^fixed' means 'not fixed', '*re*^fixed', 'fixed again'. The inflectional morphemes are meaningful too: 'fix^*ed*' signals 'past' in contrast with 'fix^*es*' which signals 'present' (and third person subject as well). Semantics is also necessarily implicated in syntax. As we saw in Chapter 3, the constituent structure 'People in Oxford/ride/bikes' means something different from 'People/ride/bikes/in Oxford'. Similarly, 'The bishop offended the actress' and 'The actress offended the bishop' are quite distinct in meaning, because word order is a syntactic device in English and so we assign subject status to the first noun phrase in each case. In both examples we have exactly the same collection of words; it is only the way they are ordered that makes them different.

The meaning of words

Facts like these have sometimes led linguists to undervalue the significance of the lexical meaning of words. It is common practice to expose the semantic indeterminacy of words in juxtaposition by citing ambiguous newspaper headlines like:

The words alone will not do, it is argued: only grammar can sort out the ambiguity by identifying different constituent structures ('settle in/well' vs 'settle/in well', for example). And the argument is often further illustrated by quoting from Lewis Carroll's 'Jabberwocky' to show the superior semantic signalling of grammar: For example,

'Twas brillig and the slithy toves
Did gyre and gimble in the wabe.

The words, it is claimed, are nonsense and so all we can do is identify the form classes on grammatical evidence: adjectives 'brillig' and 'slithy', verbs 'gyre' and 'gimble', nouns 'toves' and 'wabe'. So it is that whatever meaning can be gleaned from these lines must depend entirely on the grammar. But this does not seem to be so. Although these words are not part of the normal vocabulary of English, they resemble words that are, and so we treat them as lexical items and assign them meaning accordingly. Thus, 'brillig' can be said to suggest 'brilliant/bright', 'slithy', 'slimy/lithe', and 'wabe', 'wave'. So for me, at least, these lines project some meaning roughly on the lines of: 'It was a bright day, and reptilian creatures were frolicking in the waves'. Other people will no doubt read the lines differently, but they will do so by assigning some meaning or other to the lexical items. They will not just ignore them. Meaning may not be fully determined by lexis, but given a collection of words, as we saw with the artist and the church in Chapter 4, we can always infer *some* figment of a proposition. Grammar actually provides much less to go on. Nobody, I imagine, would make much sense of:

'Twas adjective and the adjective nouns
did verb and verb in the noun.

So although meaning is indeed signalled, as we have seen, by the morphological and syntactic processes of word adaptation and assembly, this is far from the whole story. Obviously enough these processes need words to work on, and it is the words which provide the main semantic content which is to be selected from and shaped. The grammatical processes we have discussed can be seen as playing a supportive role whereby existing units of lexical meaning are organized, modified, and tailored to requirements. They do not initiate meaning; they act upon meaning already lexically provided.

Semantic components

What kinds of meaning, then, are encoded in the word? We can begin by referring to the same principle of constituent assembly that has served us so well so far. When considering inflectional affixes in the last chapter, it was pointed out that it is common to find two morphemes fused into one form, as in 'come' + past tense = 'came'. When considering derivational affixes we noted that '*un–*' and '*re–*' can combine with various lexical items to yield others like 'unfix', 'undo', 'unscrew', 'refix', 'retell', and 'review', and so on. We have already established the semantic character of these morphological forms. We can say, then, that a lexical item like 'unfix' has two semantic elements or components, each given separate expression in the word form '*un* + fix'.

Now it happens that many such derived forms have semantic equivalents which are single morphemes: 'unwell' = 'sick', for example, 'unhappy' = 'sad'. Furthermore, there are many equivalents which can take the form not of single words but of phrases where the bound morpheme separates itself from bondage and becomes free. So 'unwell' = 'not well', 'unhappy' = 'not happy', 'reborn' = 'born again', 'replant' = 'plant again', and so on. In George Orwell's novel *1984*, this principle of decomposition provides the basis for the reformed English of Newspeak: in Newspeak, for example, 'excellent' becomes 'plusgood', 'bad' becomes 'ungood', 'terrible' becomes 'plusungood', and so on.

Now (without commitment to the principles of Newspeak) it seems reasonable to suggest that a lexical item like 'sick' is a version of 'unwell': it is just that the two morphological elements have become fused into one. It would follow that if 'unwell' has two elements of meaning or **semantic components**, then so does 'sick'. And if these lexical items can be said to be encodings of different semantic components, then it would also seem logical to suppose that the same can be said of all lexical items, the only difference being that such components are explicitly signalled in some cases, but not in others.

The signalling is not straightforward, however. When a free lexical form becomes bound as an affix, its meaning is not just added, but acts upon the host lexical item in various ways. Thus, 'careful' can be analysed as 'full of care', but 'careless' does not mean 'with less care' but 'with *no* care'. Some affixes activate grammatical relations. The suffix '*–able*', for example, contracts a passive relation with its stem. So 'eatable', for example, means not 'able to eat' but 'able *to be eaten*'. With '*–less*' and '*–able*', the semantic effect of affixation is predictable. In other cases things are not so simple. The suffix '*–er*' derives a noun from a verb, and so denotes an actor of the action. Thus, words like 'baker' and 'keeper', can be taken apart and glossed as 'a person who bakes' and 'a person who keeps (something)'. Here the actor is a human agent. But it can also be an inanimate instrument. A 'cooker' is not 'a person who cooks' but 'a device for cooking', and in words like 'printer', 'cleaner', and 'speaker' the suffix can denote either agent or instrument. And with words like 'creeper' (meaning 'plant') and 'breaker'(meaning 'wave') the original significance of the suffix has now, in part at least, disappeared.

And it is commonly the case, of course, that the distinctive meaning of the lexical host disappears and blends in with the affix in the historical process of etymological change. So it is with words like 'reckless' or 'feckless', which cannot mean 'with no reck' or ' with no feck' since there are no such lexemes in English. Conversely, when an affix attaches itself to an existing form, it may blend with its host, and again the lexical whole is not a sum of its parts. The prefix '*re–*' is even more unreliable in this respect than the suffix '*–er*' referred to above. 'Return' does not normally mean 'turn again' or 'recall' 'call again'. When they do signal such meanings, they are generally given a hyphen in writing and marked stress in speech to indicate that the prefix retains its semantic identity. Thus, you have a 're-call' ('riːkɔːl) button on the telephone, but you may not 'recall' (rɪˈkɔːl) how to use it.

The general point is, then, that we can conceive of all lexical items as encodings of one or more semantic elements or components, whether these are overtly signalled or not, and in identifying them we can establish the **denotation** of words. Thus, one denotation of the verb 'return' can be specified as [come + back], another as [give + back]. 'Come/go' and 'give/take' in turn can be said to consist of components: something along the lines of [move + self + towards/away] on the one hand, and [move + something + towards/away] on the other.

These components of meaning can be seen as analogous with segments of sound, as discussed in Chapter 4. The same principle of combination is at work. In our previous discussion, we were able to establish contrasts between phonological words by invoking minimal differences in the sequence of sound segments. Thus, 'come' (/kʌm/) contrasts with 'gum' (/gʌm/) with respect to the one feature of voice on the initial consonant—i.e. the sounds /k/ and /g/ are formed in exactly the same way, except that in /g/ the vocal cords vibrate and in /k/ they do not. The same principle applies here: we can establish similar minimal pairs of lexical items with respect to their semantic components. Thus, 'come' contrasts with 'go' in respect to the one feature of directionality: [movement + *here*] as opposed to [movement + *there*].

This approach, known as **componential analysis** thus provides an inventory of the semantic features encoded in lexical forms. It can, of course, become immensely complicated and unwieldy, and as in all analysis, as the details proliferate they can lose their point and create confusion. The essential purpose of componential analysis is to identify certain general conceptual categories or semantic principles which find expression in the particular components. Among such categories are state, process, causality, class membership, possession, dimension, location, and, as we have seen with 'come' and 'go', directionality. By invoking them, we can move on from the denotation of particular lexemes to the **sense relations** that exist between them.

Sense relations

Consider directionality, for example. As we have seen, it provides the basis for the distinction between 'come' and 'go'. But it also figures in other contrasts as well, for example, 'give/take', 'advance/retreat', 'arrive/depart', 'push/pull', 'send/receive', and 'buy/sell'. All of these pairs have the common feature of process, but the terms in each pair express opposite directionality, and in this respect are examples of **antonymy**. And within this group, we can distinguish a sub-set of which 'give/take' and 'buy/sell' are members. Here, there is a relation of reciprocal implication, known as **converseness**: 'sell' necessarily implies 'buy' and vice versa (if X sells a car to Y, Y necessarily buys the car from X). However, this sense relation is independent of directionality. Not only does it exist between the locational terms 'above/below', for example (if A is above B, B is necessarily below A), but also between such reciprocal roles as 'parent/child', where the sense and family relations, so to speak, coincide: 'If Anne is Harry's child, he is her parent'.

If we now consider a different semantic feature, that of dimension, we come to a meaning opposition (or antonym) of a rather different kind. Consider the adjective pairs: 'big/small', 'long/short', 'thin/fat', and 'far/near'. Here, we have not absolute but relative oppositeness: not either/or but degrees of difference in respect to some norm or other. Thus, a large mouse is a small animal as compared with a small elephant—or even a very small elephant—which is a large animal. Adjectives of this kind are said to be *gradable*. They can, naturally, occur with intensifiers (for example, 'very', 'extremely') and with comparative and superlative degrees (for example, 'smaller', 'smallest'). Again, as with the directional component above, this kind of antonymy is by no means restricted to lexical items with a dimensional component. 'Hot/cold', 'old/new', and 'happy/unhappy' are gradable, for example. 'Male/female', and 'married/unmarried', on the other hand, are not. You can be 'very happy' or 'rather old' but not (normally) 'rather female' or 'very married'.

The examples 'happy/unhappy', and 'married/unmarried' bring us to another sense relation. According to the earlier argument, these items with their explicit prefixes '*un–*' are equivalent in denotation to fused versions 'unhappy' = 'sad', 'unmarried' = 'single'. With the prefixed versions, the antonymy is explicitly signalled. But there are innumerable other examples where two lexical items will contract exactly the same opposition: 'buy/sell' = 'purchase/sell', 'arrive/depart' = 'arrive/leave', and so on. To the extent that 'buy' and 'purchase', and 'depart' and 'leave' are relational equivalents, they can be said to be examples of **synonymy**.

Earlier we analysed 'come' as consisting of the features [move + towards]. But 'move' as a semantic feature figures in the denotation of countless other lexical items as well of course. Thus, 'walk' is 'to move on foot'. But 'walk', too, is semantically incorporated into other words: 'march', 'amble', 'stroll', 'tramp', and 'stride', for example. 'Walk', then, is the general or **superordinate** term, and the others, the more particular instances included within it, are its subordinate terms or hyponyms. In the same way, 'animal' is a superordinate term, 'mouse' and 'elephant' are hyponyms. But we can establish intervening levels of **hyponymy**: 'mouse' is a hyponym of the superordinate 'rodent' (together with the co-hyponyms 'rat', 'porcupine', etc.), while 'rodent' is a hyponym of the superordinate 'mammal', which is in turn a hyponym of 'animal'.

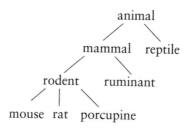

FIGURE 5.1 *Part of a hyponymic tree for 'animal'*

Each superordinate necessarily possesses a semantic feature common to all its hyponyms. To the extent that each co-hyponym has a distinct semantic specification, it serves as a superordinate to the next level of classification down, until all distinctive features are exhausted. It follows that where two lexical items appear in the same position on the tree as hyponyms we have synonymy. We may decide, for example, that 'amble' and 'stroll' are not distinguishable as ways of walking, and so are synonyms in that they have the same hyponymic relation to the superordinate word 'walk'. Notice, though, that this has to do with the equivalence of denotation as elements of the code. Synonymy as discussed here is a *semantic* relation. The extent to which synonyms have a different range of functions when they are actually put to use in contexts of communication is a different matter, which we will be taking up a little later in this chapter in the discussion of pragmatics, or meaning in context.

Relations between words

We began this chapter by looking at ways in which semantic components are overtly signalled by derivational affixes as parts of words, and we have subsequently considered how words themselves as lexical items relate semantically to others. Lexical items, however, do not only come in the form of single words. They appear as pairs, for example, in phrasal verbs ('see to', 'look up', 'pass by') or compound nouns ('prime minister', 'postage stamp', 'table lamp').

But lexical items come as larger clusters of words as well. Take the single word 'often' (morphologically simple) and the word 'repeatedly' (morphologically complex with its affixes). These can be seen as synonymous with the expressions 'over and over again' or 'time after time' respectively. Such expressions are **formulaic phrases**, and since they are complete units of meaning semantically equivalent to single words, they too can be considered as single lexical items. What distinguishes them is that in their case it happens that the semantic elements have not fused into a single form but find expression as separate words in a composite unit.

But it needs to be noticed that these lexical phrases are *compounds* of words, and not, as with the syntactic phrases that were considered in the previous section, *combinations* of words. Thus, the words in the expression 'time after time' are separate, but they are not independent as grammatical constituents. So we would not, for example, treat 'time' as a normal noun and pluralize it (*'times after times'), or add an article (**a* time after *the* time') , or replace 'after' with another preposition (**'time *before* time'). The words are compounded into a fixed association which syntax cannot meddle with. There are innumerable instances of such compounded lexical items in English, as there are in other languages: 'many a time and oft', 'by hook or by crook', 'easy come easy go', 'easier said than done', 'run of the mill', 'in the main', 'by and large', 'least said, soonest mended', and so on.

So some sequences of lexical items, or **collocations** are fixed, but there are innumerable others which are not and which *can* be syntactically modified. But only up to a point. Here, we come to the uncertain border between lexis and syntax, where words move from a compounding to a combining relationship.

Take the common expression 'He thought better of it'. Here, the subject is a normal sentence constituent and so can be replaced by an infinite number of other noun phrases ('I', 'You', 'They', 'The retired generals', 'The poor old pensioner living next door ...'). But although the noun phrase thus combines freely with what follows, the rest of the expression is resistant to replacement. It would be odd English to say: *'He reflected better of it', *'I thought worse of it', *'They thought better about it'. So this expression 'He thought better of it' consists in part of constituents which are combined and in part of lexical items which are compounded. It is not entirely fixed, as is 'by hook or by crook', for example, which is a complete lexical compound in that it admits of no interference at all (*'by the hook and the crook', *'by hooks or crooks', etc.). But it is not entirely free either, like 'He thought about it' which consists of a straightforward combination of sentence constituents. Grammatical rules can be seen as devices for regulating the meaning of words. The difficulty is that they are not completely regular in their application.

All this may seem to be fairly trivial—a detail or two about the peculiarities of English. But it illustrates again that semantics is not only a matter of assigning meaning to individual units, whether these be morphemes or words, but is also concerned with the *relationships* between them, how they act upon each other, how they fuse, compound, and combine in different ways. Semantics is the complex interplay of morphology, lexis, and syntax. Complex though it is, however, it does not account for all aspects of meaning. We still have pragmatics to consider.

Meaning in context: pragmatics

Semantics is the study of meaning *in* language. It is concerned with what language means. This is not the same as what people mean *by* the language they use, how they actualize its meaning potential as a communicative resource. This is the concern of **pragmatics**.

The distinction is easy enough to demonstrate. Consider the expression:

The parson may object to it.

Our knowledge of the English language suffices for us to decipher this as a sentence. We know that the symbol 'the' is a definite article denoting shared knowledge and contracting a sense relation with other terms in the determiner system ('the parson' as distinct from 'a parson' or 'this/that parson'). We know that the noun 'parson' denotes a particular religious office, is hyponym to the superordinate 'clergyman' (together with other terms like 'priest', 'rector', 'bishop', and so on). We know how the phrase 'the parson' functions as a constituent, and we identify 'may' as a modal constituent of the verb phrase. With knowledge of this kind, we recognize this expression as a syntactically complete *sentence* and assign it semantic meaning accordingly. But for all this, we do not know what might be meant by the expression in an actual *utterance*, that is to say, when we hear it or read it in a specific context.

Let us imagine somebody coming out with the expression as a remark in the context of a conversation. What kinds of thing might they mean by it? We can *decipher the sentence* by invoking semantic criteria, but how do we *interpret the utterance*?

Reference, force, and effect

Consider the first phrase 'The parson'. The use of the definite article points us in the direction of a particular clergyman assumed to be known about by both speaker and hearer. The noun phrase, then, now takes on a 'pointing' or 'indexical' function, and as such becomes communicatively active as **reference**. But we, as second person parties, have to ratify the reference of course. If we know of no such individual, then the definite article simply directs us into a void, and is indexically invalid ('Parson? Which parson?').

One kind of pragmatic meaning we can assign to an utterance, then, is that of reference. The speaker is talking about something, expressing a **proposition** by using the symbolic conventions of the code to key us into a context of shared knowledge. But the speaker is not just talking about something, but is doing so in order to perform some kind of **illocution** or communicative act. The utterance not only has reference but also **illocutionary force**. So the speaker may intend 'The parson may object to it' as a reason for a decision taken, or as an objection to a particular course of action, or as a warning. 'The parson may object to it.'—'Thanks for telling me.' These pragmatic possibilities are not signalled in the language itself: they again have to be inferred from the context in which the utterance is made.

One aspect of pragmatic meaning, then, is (propositional) reference, another is (illocutionary) force. There is a third we can identify. In making an utterance, the first person party expresses a certain intended meaning designed not just to be understood as such, but to have some kind of effect on the second person: to frighten, or persuade, or impress, or establish a sense of common purpose or shared concern. ('The parson may object to it.'—'Oh my God!'). This is known as **perlocutionary effect**.

Context and schema

When we talk about propositional reference, illocutionary force, and perlocutionary effect, we are dealing not with the semantic meaning as encoded in the language itself, but the pragmatic meaning which people achieve in **speech acts**.

With speech acts we are again concerned with relationships, but this time not those which are internal to the language itself, but those between aspects of the language and aspects of the external circumstances in which it is used on a particular occasion, its context of occurrence. This context is not just reality in the raw, but those aspects of it which are recognized as significant. Here, we need to invoke again the basic principles of classification which have already been applied. It was pointed out in Chapter 3 that speakers of a language discriminate sounds as phonemically significant by filtering out certain phonetic features. These are not heard as meaningful and so they do not count. In this respect, speakers project their own pattern of reality. The same principle applies to context. When people make an indexical connection, they do so by linking features of the language with familiar features of their world, with what is established in their minds as a normal pattern of reality or **schema**. In other words, context is a schematic construct. It is not 'out there', so to speak, but in the mind. So the achievement of pragmatic meaning is a matter of matching up the linguistic elements of the code with the schematic elements of the context. So, for example, if you were to hear someone make the remark 'Brazil scored just before the final whistle', the likelihood is that the word 'Brazil' would not call to mind the Amazonian rain forests, coffee, or Copacabana Beach (schematic associations which might be relevant on other contextual occasions), but a football team celebrated for its skill. The football schema thus engaged would lead you to infer what the expressions 'scored' and 'final whistle' referred to among all the possibilities that they *might* refer to in other contexts.

Consider again the comment about the parson. Reference is made to a particular clergyman assumed to be known to both parties. But what is it about him that is relevant here? The 'it' that he might object to could call up the schema associated with his ecclesiastical office: it might refer, for example, to putting a TV in the vestry, replacing the choir with a pop group, using church funds to buy lottery tickets, and so on. What is relevant here is the parson's role as clergyman and custodian of the values of his religion rather than the fact that he is overweight, or near retirement, or unmarried, or plays golf, or rides a bicycle, or smokes a pipe, or whatever. But any one of these *could* be contextually relevant, of course. Everything depends on what 'it' refers to. Reference is achieved when both speaker and hearer engage the same context by converging on what is schematically relevant.

The same thing applies to the achievement of force. The utterance, it was suggested, could be taken as a warning. How might such a force be inferred? Again, the notion of schema comes in. People in a particular community have common assumptions not only about the way the world is organized, but also about the customary ways that social actions like speech acts are performed. It is just these common assumptions that define their cultural identity as members of a social group, small or large. So, in this case, the people in this interaction know that for an utterance to count as the illocutionary act of warning it has to meet certain conditions. To begin with, it obviously has to make reference to some possible future event which would be in some way against the interests of the hearer. But both these conditions apply to the illocutionary act of threat as well. What distinguishes the two is that in the case of a threat, the future event is within the power of the first person to bring about, whereas with a warning it is not.

What then of the parson? If the person whom the utterance is addressed knows that the speaker is on the parson's side, has influence over him, indeed speaks for him, then this will be the relevant feature about him, the context thereby meets the required condition for the utterance to function as a threat. If, on the other hand, the hearer knows that the speaker does not make common cause with the parson, but sees him as an outside influence over which he, the speaker, has no control, then the utterance will be taken as a warning.

Negotiation of meaning

It may be, of course, that it is unclear whether the context meets one condition or another, whether it is a warning or a threat, and this creates ambiguity. The hearer may eliminate all kinds of circumstantial information as irrelevant to context, but still be left with evidence for more than one possible interpretation. This potential ambiguity applies to all the aspects of pragmatic meaning that we have touched on: reference and effect as well as force. So interpretation commonly involves the parties concerned in the negotiation of meaning, whereby an agreed frame of reference or set of illocutionary conditions is established. One might imagine interactions along the following lines:

A: The parson may object to it.
B: Parson? Which parson?
A: The Reverend Spooner.
B: But he isn't a member. And he doesn't smoke anyway.
A: What's that got to do with the new bicycle shed?
B: I thought you were talking about the smoking ban.

A: The parson may object to it.
B: I don't think we need worry about that.
A: Well perhaps you should. As the chair I must tell you that he will have my support.
B: Yes, and we all know why.
A: That remark is out of order and I must ask you to withdraw it.
B: Don't be such a pompous ass.

A number of other matters arise from these exchanges. Firstly, they are presented here as a written record of an imagined interaction: that is to say, as the text of a supposed discourse. We must assume that many features of such a discourse would remain unrecorded: **paralinguistic** features, for example, like tones of voice, gesture, facial expression, eye contact, and so on, which might well be contextually relevant and indeed crucial for understanding what is going on. Even if we had recourse to sound tape and video, what would be recorded would be the textual product of the interaction, and not the actual process of the discourse as experienced by the participants.

Secondly, although we began our discussion, as we have in earlier chapters, with simple units of meaning, we are drawn inevitably into a consideration of more complex ones. Although we demonstrated the basic kinds of pragmatic meaning by invoking the speech act as an individual utterance, a kind of pragmatic version of the semantic sentence, it is clear that communication does not take place by the neat sequence of such speech acts. In the first place, they frequently call for negotiation, as we have seen, whereby first person intention and second person interpretation are brought to some satisfactory degree of convergence. Meaning is jointly managed in spoken interaction by turn taking, the sharing of the floor, with different participants assuming the first person speaker role of adjusting the setting for the continuation of the interaction. A major concern of pragmatics is how discourse is managed, what the ground rules for negotiation are, and how (and how far) the different parties cooperate in this joint enterprise. Clearly, when people seek to communicate, they enter into a kind of contract that they will work towards some convergence of intention and interpretation, that is to say, they subscribe to a **cooperative principle**. Otherwise, there would be no way for the semantic potential of language to be given any pragmatic realization at all. There has to be some agreement that what people mean by what they say can be related to what, by established semantic convention, the language itself means. This is not to say that the discourse that people enact will always result in a convergence of *opinion*. Cooperation does not preclude conflict. Indeed, it is only by subscribing to the cooperative principle that people can express disagreement or create conflictual situations.

Relations between utterances

Obviously for any communication to take place, the two parties need to share a common linguistic code (i.e. to speak the same language), but equally they have to be willing, and able, to draw upon it in accordance with normal communicative conventions. Thus, in our second sample interaction, there is clearly a confrontation developing between A and B. But that very confrontation depends on both parties conforming to the semantic conventions of English as their common code, and also to certain pragmatic conventions which regulate the way the code is used. There are, for example, very general conventions of **cohesion** which establish referential links across the utterances. So it is that each of the interactants recognizes, for example, that 'it' and 'that' refer back to specific things said earlier, that 'you should' and 'we all know why' are reduced or elliptical expressions which are completed by reference to the preceding utterance.

There are also general **turn-taking** conventions which regulate the interaction itself. One of these is the recognition that a pause signals the end of a turn in conversation and an optional shift of speaker role to the second person. Another convention not only constrains the shift of turn but determines what *kind* of turn the second person is to take. So it is, for example, that in asking a question I concede my turn and give you the right to reply. A response is conventionally required. In this respect, question and answer are dependent parts of a single exchange and constitute what is called an **adjacency pair**.

These are very general conventions which regulate the relationship between utterances, but there are more specific ones as well which define how speech acts combine in different modes of communication, or **genres**. The second of the interactions we have been considering, for example, has some of the features of a formal meeting. A convention of this genre is that authority is vested in a chairperson who has the power to control turn-taking and regulate what is said. This accounts for A's statement: 'That remark is out of order and I must ask you to withdraw it.' How, then, do we account for B's reply 'Don't be such a pompous ass'? He may not know the conventions of this particular genre: in other words its formal procedures may not be part of his schematic knowledge. Or it may be that he knows them well enough but chooses to challenge them, seeking to assert a position other than that which A, the chairperson, wants to submit him to.

This illustrates a very general point about pragmatics. It is concerned in part with how language engages the schematic knowledge people have of what is normal and customary in their particular communities. In this respect pragmatics is the study of how people conform to social conventions. But it is also concerned with the ways such conventions can be circumvented or subverted by individual initiative. Uses of language are, in one respect, necessarily acts of conformity. But they are not only that: they are also acts of identity whereby people assert themselves and manipulate others. Pragmatics is concerned with how people negotiate meaning but also how they negotiate social relations.

And we should note that pragmatics is as much concerned with written as with spoken uses of language. The conventions which come into play for communication and control apply here too. First person writers assume a degree of shared schematic knowledge, produce texts which are cohesive and which conform to the conventions of a particular genre. They count on their readers to cooperate in inferring the values of reference, force, and effect that they intend. To be sure, there can be no immediate reciprocal negotiation of meaning, no joint management of the interaction as there is in conversations. The writer, in sole control, has to make projections about possible readers and anticipate their reactions, thereby enacting a discourse by proxy so to speak, and providing a text as a partial record of it. The readers then have to use the text to activate a discourse of their own, cooperating with the writer as far as they are able or willing to do. In written uses of language, then, the interaction between first and second person parties is displaced and the negotiation of meaning is carried out in two stages. But the meaning is negotiable none the less. It is not inscribed in the language itself and so texts do not signal their own significance. With writing as with speech, pragmatics is concerned with what people *make* of their language.

6
Current issues

Linguistics, like language itself, is dynamic and therefore subject to change. It would lose its validity otherwise, for like all areas of intellectual enquiry, it is continually questioning established ideas and questing after new insights. That is what enquiry means. Its very nature implies a degree of instability. So although there is, in linguistics, a reasonably secure conceptual common ground, which this book has sought to map out, there is, beyond that, a variety of different competing theories, different visions and revisions, disagreements and disputes, about what the scope and purpose of the discipline should be. There are three related issues which are particularly prominent in current debate. One has to do with the very definition of the discipline and takes us back to the question of idealization discussed in Chapter 2. Another issue concerns the nature of linguistic data and has come into prominence with the development of computer programs for the analysis of large corpora of language. A third issue raises the question of accountability and the extent to which linguistic enquiry should be made relevant to the practical problems of everyday life.

The scope of linguistics

As was pointed out in Chapter 2, linguistics has traditionally been based on an idealization which abstracts the formal properties of the language code from the contextual circumstances of actual instances of use, seeking to identify some relatively stable linguistic knowledge (*langue*, or competence) which underlies the vast variety of linguistic behaviour (*parole*, or performance). It was also pointed out that there are two reasons for idealizing to such a degree of abstraction. One has to do with practical *feasibility*: it is convenient to idealize in this way because the actuality of language behaviour is too elusive to capture by any significant generalization. But the other reason has to do with theoretical *validity*, and it is this which motivates Chomsky's competence–performance distinction. The position here is that the data of actual behaviour are disregarded not because they are elusive but because they are of little real theoretical interest: they do not provide reliable evidence for the essential nature of human language. Over recent years, this formalist definition of the scope of linguistics has been challenged with respect to both feasibility and validity.

As far as feasibility is concerned, it has been demonstrated that the data of behaviour are not so resistant to systematic account as they were made out to be. There are two aspects of behaviour. One is psychological and concerns how linguistic knowledge is organized for access and what the accessing processes might be in both the acquisition and use of language. This has been a subject of enquiry in **psycholinguistics**. The second aspect of behaviour is sociological. This accessing of linguistic knowledge is prompted by some communicative need, some social context which calls for an appropriate use of language. These conditions for appropriateness can be specified, as indeed was demonstrated in part in the discussion of pragmatics in Chapter 5. The account of the relationship between linguistic code and social context is the business of **sociolinguistics**.

Psycholinguistic work on accessing processes and sociolinguistic work on appropriateness conditions have demonstrated that there are aspects of behaviour that can be systematically studied, and that rigorous enquiry does not depend on the high degree of abstraction proposed in formalist linguistics. In other words, psycholinguistics and sociolinguistics have things to say about language which are also within the legitimate scope of the discipline. Such a point of view would be a tolerant and neighbourly one: we stake out different areas of language study, each with its own legitimacy.

But the challenge to the formalist approach in respect to validity is quite different. It is not tolerant and neighbourly at all, but a matter of competing claims for the same territory. It is not just an issue of delimitation but of definition, and proposes a **functionalist** one in opposition to a formalist one. The argument here is that it diminishes the very study of language to reduce it to abstract forms because to do so is to eliminate from consideration just about everything that is really significant about it and to make it hopelessly remote from people's actual experience. Language, the argument goes, is not essentially a static and well-defined cognitive construct but a mode of communication which is intrinsically dynamic and unstable. Its forms are of significance only so far as we can associate them with their communicative functions. On this account, the only valid linguistics is **functional linguistics**.

But, as was indicated in Chapter 2, there are two senses in which linguistic forms can be said to be associated with functions, and therefore two ways of defining functional linguistics. Firstly, we can consider how the linguistic code has developed in response to the uses to which it is put. In this sense, functional linguistics is the study of how the formal properties of language are *informed* by the functions it serves, how it encodes perceptions of reality, ways of thinking, cultural values, and so on.

Secondly, we can think of the form–function association as a matter not of encoded meaning potential but of its actual realization in communication; and here we are concerned with the way language forms function *pragmatically* in different contexts of use. In this case formalist linguistics is challenged not because it defines the language code too narrowly without regard to the social factors which have formed it, but because it defines language *only* in reference to the code, without regard to how it is put to use in communication. The argument here is that linguistics should extend its scope to account not only for the knowledge of the internalized language of the code, or linguistic competence, but for the knowledge people have of how this is appropriately acted upon, or communicative competence.

These two senses of functional linguistics are frequently confused, and there has sometimes been a tendency to suppose that if you define the code in reference to the communicative functions that have influenced its formation over time, then it follows that you will automatically be accounting for the way in which the code functions in communication here and now. But to do this is to equate the *semantic potential* of the code with actual *pragmatic realizations* of it in communication.

Functional linguistics, in both senses, considers language as an essentially social phenomenon, designed for communication. There is no interest in what makes human language a species-specific endowment, in those universal features of language which might provide evidence of innateness which were described in Chapter 1. The concerns of functional linguistics are closer in this respect to the reality of language as people experience it, and it is therefore often seen as more likely than **formal linguistics** to be applicable to the problems of everyday life. Opponents might argue that this is only achieved at the expense of theoretical rigour. This raises the general question of how far relevance and accountability are valid considerations in linguistic enquiry, and this will be taken up again a little later. It also raises the question of what the source of linguistic data should be, and it is to this matter that we now turn.

The data of linguistics

There are, broadly speaking, three sources of linguistic data we can draw upon to infer facts about language. We can, to begin with, use *introspection*, appealing to our own intuitive competence as the data source. This is a tradition in linguistics of long standing, and essentially makes operational Saussure's concept of *langue* as common knowledge, imprinted in the mind like a book of which all members of the community have identical copies. So if linguists want data, as representative members of a language community they have only to consult the copy in their head. Most grammars and dictionaries until recent times have been based on this assumption that linguistic description can be drawn from the linguist's introspection. And it is not only linguistic competence which is accessible to introspection, but communicative competence as well, so the argument is that the conventions that define appropriate language use can also be drawn from the same intuitive source.

If, however, there is some reason to doubt the representative nature of such intuitive sampling, there is a second way of getting at data, namely by *elicitation.* In this case, you use other members of the community as informants, drawing on *their* intuitions. And again, this might be directed at obtaining the data of the code or its communicative use. Thus, you might ask informants whether a particular combination of linguistic elements are grammatically possible in their language, or what would be an appropriate expression given a particular context.

Introspection and elicitation can be used to establish both the formal properties of a language and how they typically function in use. But in both cases the data is abstract knowledge, and not actual behaviour. They reveal what people know about what they do but not what they actually do. If you want data of that kind, the data of performance rather than competence, you need to turn to *observation*.   ③

The development of computer technology over recent years has made observation possible on a vast scale. Programs have been devised within **corpus linguistics** to collect and analyse large corpora of actually occurring language, both written and spoken, and this analysis reveals facts about the frequency and co-occurrence of lexical and grammatical items which are not intuitively accessible by introspection or elicitation.

It would seem on the face of it that this is a much more reliable source of data. It is surely better to find out what people actually do than depend on intuitions which are often uncertain and contradictory. Claims have indeed been made that these large-scale observations reveal patterns of attested usage which call for a complete revision of the existing categories of linguistic description, which are generally based on intuition and elicitation. Corpus linguistics, in dealing with actual behaviour, clearly has an affinity with functional linguistics in that it too claims to get closer to the facts of 'real' language.

There is no doubt that corpus analysis can reveal facts of usage, the data of actual linguistic performance, which throw doubt on the validity of any model of language based on the idea of a stable and well-defined system. The elaborate picture it presents is very different from the abstract painting proposed by the formal linguist. If language use is indeed a rule-governed activity, as is often said, the rules are not easy to discern in the detail. And it is also true that this detail is not accessible to introspection or elicitation. Even a limited corpus analysis can show patterns of occurrence of which language users, the very producers of the data, are unaware. Corpus linguistics transcends intuitive knowledge and in this respect can be seen as a valuable, and valid, corrective to unfounded abstraction: a case of description influencing theory for once, rather than the other way round.

But the claims of corpus linguistics can be questioned too. The facts of usage revealed by computer analysis, for example, carry no guarantee of absolute truth. The intuitions that people have about their language have their own validity as data. These conceptual constructs are also real, but the reality is of a different order.

One example of this is the way lexical knowledge (in some areas of vocabulary at least) seems to be organized semantically in terms of **prototypes**, and these cannot be observed, but only elicited. Thus, when a group of English-speaking informants were asked to give the first example that came to mind of a more inclusive category of things they showed a striking unanimity. The word 'bird' elicited 'robin' (rather than, say, 'chaffinch' or 'wren') and the word 'vegetable' elicited 'pea' (rather than, say, 'parsnip' or 'potato'). For these informants, then, a robin is the prototypical bird, a pea the prototypical vegetable. But this conceptual preference does not correspond with how frequently these words actually occur in a corpus. The same point can be made about grammatical structures. If English-speaking informants are asked to provide examples of a sentence, they are likely to come up with simple subject–verb–object (SVO) constructions ('The man opened the door'; 'John kissed Mary'). These, we might say, are prototypical English sentences. But they are unlikely to figure very frequently in a corpus of actual usage. Since people do not use simple sentences like this very often, they do not have much reality as observed data, but they may have a significant psychological reality nevertheless. They may be evidence of competence which is not reflected in the facts of performance.

Prototypes thus elicited do not, of course, invalidate the observed data of corpus linguistics. They provide a different kind of data which are evidence of competence which is not directly projected into performance. Intuitive, elicited, and observed data all have their own validity, but this validity depends on what kind of evidence you are looking for, on what aspects of language knowledge or behaviour you are seeking to explain. If you are looking for evidence of the internal relationship between language and the mind, you are more likely to favour intuition and elicitation. If you are looking for evidence of how language sets up external links with society, then you are more likely to look to the observed data of actual occurrence. The validity of different kinds of linguistic data is not absolute but relative: one kind is no more 'real' than another. It depends on what you claim the data are evidence of, and what you are trying to explain.

The relevance of linguistics

From questions of validity we turn now to questions of utility. What is linguistics *for*? What good is it to anybody? What practical uses can it be put to? One response to such questions is, of course, to deny the presupposition that it needs any practical justification at all. Like other disciplines, linguistics is an intellectual enquiry, a quest for explanation, and that is sufficient justification in itself. Understanding does not have to be accountable to practical utility, particularly when it concerns the nature of language, which, as was indicated in Chapter 1, is so essential and distinctive a feature of the human species.

Whether or not linguistics *should* be accountable, it has been turned to practical account. Indeed, one important impetus for the development of linguistics in the first part of this century was the dedicated work done in translating the Bible into languages hitherto unwritten and undescribed. This practical task implied a prior exercise in **descriptive linguistics**, since it involved the analysis of the languages (through elicitation and observation) into which the scriptures were to be rendered. And this necessarily called for a continual reconsideration of established linguistic categories to ensure that they were relevant to languages other than those, like English, upon which they were originally based. The practical tasks of description and translation inevitably raised issues of wider theoretical import.

They raise other issues as well about the relationship between theory and practice and the role of the linguist, issues which are of current relevance in other areas of enquiry, and which bear upon the relationship between descriptive and **applied linguistics**.

The process of translation involves the interpretation of a text encoded in one language and the rendering of it into another text which, though necessarily different in form, is, as far as possible, equivalent in meaning. In so far as it raises questions about the differences between language codes it can be seen as an exercise in **contrastive analysis**. In so far as it raises questions about the meaning of particular texts, particular communicative uses of the codes, it can be seen as an exercise in **discourse analysis**. Both of these areas of enquiry have laid claim to practical relevance and so to be the business of applied linguistics.

With regard to contrastive analysis, one obvious area of application is language teaching. After all, second language learning, like translation, has to do with working out relationships between one language and another: the first language (L1) you know and the second language (L2) you do not. It seems self-evident that the points of difference between the two codes will constitute areas of difficulty for learners and that a contrastive analysis will therefore be of service in the design of a teaching programme.

It turns out, however, that the findings of such analysis cannot be directly applied in this way. Although learners do undoubtedly refer the second language they are learning (L2) to their own mother tongue (L1), in effect using translation as a strategy for learning, they do not do so in any regular or predictable manner. Linguistic *difference* is not a reliable measure of learning *difficulty*. The data of actual learner performance, as established by **error analysis,** call for an alternative theoretical explanation.

One possibility is that learners conform to a pre-programmed cognitive agenda and so acquire features of language in a particular order of acquisition. In this way they proceed through different interim stages of an **interlanguage** which is unique to the acquisition process itself. Enquiry into this possibility in **Second Language Acquisition (SLA)** research has been extensive.

There is another possibility. It might be that the categories of description typically used in contrastive analysis are not sufficiently sensitive to record certain aspects of learner language. Learners may be influenced by features of their L1 experience other than the most obvious forms of the code. Contrastive analysis has been mainly concerned with syntactic structure, but as we have seen in Chapters 4 and 5, this is only one aspect of language, and one which, furthermore, inter-relates with others in complex ways. So it may be that the learners' difficulties do correspond to differences between their L1 and L2, but that we need a more sophisticated theory to discern what the differences are, a theory which takes a more comprehensive view of the nature of language by taking discourse into account.

Discourse analysis is potentially relevant to the problems of language pedagogy in two other ways. Firstly, it can provide a means of describing the eventual goal of learning, the ability to communicate, and so to cope with the conventions of use associated with certain discourses, written or spoken. Secondly, it can provide the means of describing the contexts which are set up in classrooms to induce the process of learning. In this case it can provide a basis for classroom research.

But the relevance of discourse analysis is not confined to language teaching. It can be used to investigate how language is used to sustain social institutions and manipulate opinion; how it is used in the expression of ideology and the exercise of power. Such investigations in **critical discourse analysis** seek to raise awareness of the social significance and the political implications of language use. Discourse analysis can also be directed to developing awareness of the significance of linguistic features in the interpretation of literary texts, the particular concern of **stylistics**.

In these and other cases, descriptive linguistics becomes applied linguistics to the extent that the descriptions can be shown to be relevant to an understanding of practical concerns associated with language use and learning. These concerns may take the form of quite specific problems: how to design a literacy programme, for example, or how to interpret linguistic evidence in a court of law (the concern of the growing field of **forensic linguistics**).

But other concerns for relevance are more general and more broadly educational. We began this book by noting how thoroughly language pervades our reality, how central it is to our lives as individuals and social beings. To remain unaware of it what it is and how it works is to run the risk of being deprived or exploited. Control of language is, to a considerable degree, control of power. Language is too important a human resource for its understanding to be kept confined to linguists. Language is so implicated in human life that we need to be as fully aware of it as possible, for otherwise we remain in ignorance of what constitutes our essential humanity.

SECTION 2
Readings

Chapter 1
The nature of language

Text 1

JOHN LYONS: *Language and Linguistics: An Introduction.*
Cambridge University Press 1981, pages 19–21

*The following text deals with the design features of language:
those features of human language which distinguish it from
other forms of communication (see Chapter 1, pages 4–8).
One such feature is arbitrariness: linguistic signs do not
resemble the things they refer to. Another is duality: elements
at one level combine to form units at a higher level, and
for this to happen, the elements have to be discrete. These
properties together provide language with its distinctive productivity.*

Perhaps the most striking characteristic of language by comparison with other codes or communication-systems is its flexibility
and versatility. We can use language to give vent to our emotions
and feelings; to solicit the co-operation of our fellows; to make
threats or promises; to issue commands, ask questions or make
statements. We can make reference to the past, present and
future; to things far removed from the situation of utterance—
even to things that need not exist and could not exist. No other
system of communication, human or non-human, would seem to
have anything like the same degree of flexibility and versatility.
Among the more specific properties that contribute to the flexibility and versatility of language (i.e. of each and every language-

system), there are four that have frequently been singled out for mention: arbitrariness, duality, discreteness and productivity. ...

...The most obvious instance of ARBITRARINESS in language—and the one that is most frequently mentioned—has to do with the link between form and meaning, between the signal and the message. There are sporadic instances in all languages of what is traditionally referred to as onomatopoeia: cf. the non-arbitrary connection between the form and the meaning of such onomatopoeic words as 'cuckoo', 'peewit', 'crash', in English. But the vast majority of the words in all languages are non-onomatopoeic: the connection between their form and their meaning is arbitrary in that, given the form, it is impossible to predict the meaning and, given the meaning, it is impossible to predict the form.

▷ *Can you think of other words in English (or in any other language) which are onomatopoeic?*

▷ *Do you think that onomatopeia, as illustrated here, does in fact indicate a non-arbitrary relationship between form and meaning? Try getting colleagues to predict the meaning of onomatopoeic words in languages unfamiliar to them.*

... By DUALITY is meant the property of having two LEVELS of structure, such that units of the primary level are composed of ELEMENTS of the secondary level and each of the two levels has its own principles of organization. ...

... we can think of the elements of spoken language as sounds ... The sounds do not of themselves convey meaning. Their sole function is to combine with one another to make units which do, in general, have a particular meaning. It is because the smaller, lower-level elements are meaningless whereas the larger, higher-level, units generally, if not invariably, have a distinct and identifiable meaning that the elements are described as secondary and the units as primary. All communication-systems have such primary units; but these units are not necessarily made up of elements. It is only if a system has both units and elements that it has the property of duality. ...

▷ *If the elements of spoken language are sounds, what are the elements of written language? Do they combine into higher level units in the same way?*

▷ *Primary level sounds combine to form secondary level words.*
But words also combine to form larger units, namely sen-
tences. So is the relationship between the levels of sound and
word the same as that between word and sentence?

DISCRETENESS is opposed to continuity, or continuous variation. In the case of language, discreteness is a property of the secondary elements. To illustrate: the two words 'bit' and 'bet' differ
in form, in both the written and the spoken language. It is quite
possible to produce a vowel-sound that is half-way between the
vowels that normally occur in the pronunciation of these two
words. But if we substitute this intermediate sound for the vowel
of 'bit' or 'bet' in the same context, we shall not thereby have pronounced some third word distinct from either or sharing the characteristics of both. We shall have pronounced something that is
not recognized as a word at all or, alternatively, something that is
identified as a mispronounced version of one or the other. Identity
of form in language is, in general, a matter of all or nothing, not of
more or less. ...

... The productivity of a communication-system is the property
which makes possible the construction and interpretation of new
signals: i.e. of signals that have not been previously encountered
and are not found on some list—however large that list might
be—of prefabricated signals, to which the user has access.

▷ *Do you see any logical relationships among the design fea-*
tures discussed here? Do you think that the discreteness of
language depends, for example, on the fact that it is arbitrary?

Text 2
B.L.WHORF: *Language, Thought and Reality: Selected*
Writings. MIT Press 1956, page 215

If the connection between the form and meaning of linguistic
signs is arbitrary and established only by convention, it would
seem to follow that the way we see the world is in some degree
determined by this convention. Language is not dependent on
reality, but perhaps reality is dependent on language?

... In English we divide most of our words into two classes, which
have different grammatical and logical properties. Class 1 we call

nouns, e.g., 'house, man'; class 2 verbs, e.g., 'hit, run'. Many words of one class can act secondarily as of the other class, e.g., 'a hit, a run', or 'to man (the boat')), but, on the primary level, the division between the classes is absolute. Our language thus gives us a bipolar division of nature. But nature herself is not thus polarized. If it be said that 'strike, turn, run,' are verbs because they denote temporary or short-lasting events, i.e., actions, why then is 'fist' a noun? It also is a temporary event. Why are 'lightning, spark, wave, eddy, pulsation, flame, storm, phase, cycle, spasm, noise, emotion' nouns? They are temporary events. If 'man' and 'house' are nouns because they are long-lasting and stable events, i.e., things, what then are 'keep, adhere, extend, project, continue, persist, grow, dwell', and so on doing among the verbs? If it be objected that 'possess, adhere' are verbs because they are stable relationships rather than stable percepts, why then should 'equilibrium, pressure, current, peace, group, nation, society, tribe, sister,' or any kinship term be among the nouns? It will be found that an 'event' to us means 'what our language classes as a verb' or something analogized therefrom. And it will be found that it is not possible to define 'event, thing, object relationship', and so on, from nature, but that to define them always involves a circuitous return to the grammatical categories of the definer's language.

▷ *What do you think is the relationship between the arbitrariness of the linguistic sign and the way language is used to classify reality?*

▷ *Whorf's examples here are all from English. Can you provide examples from other languages which prove (or disprove) the point he is making?*

Text 3

VICTORIA A. FROMKIN and ROBERT RODMAN:
An Introduction to Language (5th edn.) Harcourt Brace Jovanovich 1993, page 27

Text 1 referred to the design features of arbitrariness, duality, discreteness, and productivity. The following text makes no mention of any of these by name, even though it deals with what is distinctive about human language, especially its creativity. These design features can be seen as providing for this.

If language is defined merely as a system of communication, then language is not unique to humans. There are, however, certain characteristics of human language not found in the communication systems of any other species. A basic property of human language is its CREATIVE ASPECT—a speaker's ability to combine the basic linguistic units to form an *infinite* set of 'well-formed' grammatical sentences, most of which are novel, never before produced or heard.

The fact that deaf children learn language shows that the ability to hear or produce sounds is not a necessary prerequisite for language learning. Further, the ability to imitate the sounds of human language is not a sufficient basis for learning language; 'talking' birds imitate sounds but can neither segment these sounds into smaller units, nor understand what they are imitating, nor produce new utterances to convey their thoughts.

Birds, bees, crabs, spiders, and most other creatures communicate in some way, but the information imparted is severely limited and stimulus-bound, confined to a small set of messages. The system of language represented by intricate mental grammars, which are not stimulus-bound and which generate infinite messages, is unique to the human species.

▷ *The 'creative aspect' of human language is described as 'a speaker's ability to combine the basic linguistic units to form an infinite set of "well-formed" grammatical sentences'. How far is this accounted for by the design features discussed in Text 1?*

▷ *Why do you think the writers use inverted commas in the expression 'talking' birds?*

▷ *What do you think the writer means by saying that the communication of other creatures is 'stimulus-bound'?*

Text 4

RONALD WARDHAUGH: *Investigating Language: Central Problems in Linguistics*. Blackwell 1993, pages 64–5

The speaking activity is not the same as the language ability (as witness the 'talking' birds in Text 3). It is the language ability (it is claimed) which is specific to the human species, and which all humans therefore have in common (see Chapter 1, pages 8–10). If so, then it would seem to follow that different languages must also have something in common.

Speaking itself as an activity often looms large in definitions of language, as is deciding whether or not any other species is capable of acquiring language. But language ability is more than just the use of speech; it involves the complex manipulation of sets of signs. It is quite obvious that species other than the human species can manipulate signs and engage in complex forms of signing behaviour. What is crucial in this regard is whether any other species has the capacity to handle the syntactic organization of human signing in which finite systems of principles and operations allow users to create sentences out of an infinite set of possibilities. Only humans appear to have this capacity; it is almost certainly species-specific.

One consequence is that all languages are alike in certain respects, all children acquire language in very much the same way and all languages are equally easy—or difficult—for those who acquire them as children. Everyone learns a language and uses it in much the same way for much the same purposes and with relatively little variation in either time or space. If this is so, language is inherently different from any kind of communication system found in any other species.

▷ *One consequence [of language ability being species-specific] is that all languages are alike in certain respects …'. How is this a consequence? Alike in what respects? What shows that 'language is inherently different from any other kind of communication system found in any other species'?*

Text 5

NOAM CHOMSKY: *Reflections on Language.* Pantheon Books 1975, pages 3–4

If language is something unique to the human species, a genetic endowment (see Chapter 1, pages 11–13) then one reason for studying it is that it provides evidence of the universal features of the human mind ('the mental characteristics of the species'). And this, in turn, leads to an explanation of how children can acquire it so effortlessly.

Why study language? There are many possible answers, and by focusing on some I do not, of course, mean to disparage others or question their legitimacy. One may, for example, simply be fascinated by the elements of language in themselves and want to discover their order and arrangement, their origin in history or in the individual, or the ways in which they are used in thought, in science or in art, or in normal social interchange. One reason for studying language—and for me personally the most compelling reason—is that it is tempting to regard language, in the traditional phrase, as 'a mirror of mind'. I do not mean by this simply that the concepts expressed and distinctions developed in normal language use give us insight into the patterns of thought and the world of 'common sense' constructed by the human mind. More intriguing, to me at least, is the possibility that by studying language we may discover abstract principles that govern its structure and use, principles that are universal by biological necessity and not mere historical accident, that derive from mental characteristics of the species. A human language is a system of remarkable complexity. To come to know a human language would be an extraordinary intellectual achievement for a creature not specifically designed to accomplish this task. A normal child acquires this knowledge on relatively slight exposure and without specific training. He can then quite effortlessly make use of an intricate structure of specific rules and guiding principles to convey his thoughts and feelings to others, arousing in them novel ideas and subtle perceptions and judgments. For the conscious mind, not specially designed for the purpose, it remains a distant goal to reconstruct and comprehend what the child has done intuitively and with minimal effort. Thus language is a mirror of mind in a deep and significant sense. It is a product of human intelligence, created anew in each individual by operations that lie far beyond the reach of will or consciousness.

▷ *In previous texts, the design features of human language have been given as evidence that it is species-specific. Are these features the same, then, as the 'abstract principles' that Chomsky refers to here?*

▷ *Chomsky refers to language as an 'intellectual achievement' and 'a product of human intelligence' but something which*

*the child acquires 'intuitively and with minimal effort'. Is
there a contradiction here? And if not, why not?*

Text 6

M.A.K. HALLIDAY: 'Language structure and language
function' in John Lyons (ed.): *New Horizons in Linguistics.*
Penguin 1970, pages 142–3

*Chomsky's reason for studying language is psychological: it is
because the form it takes derives from universal principles of
the human mind. Halliday's reason, as outlined in the following text, is sociological: in his view, the form language takes as
a system of signs (or semiotic) depends on the social functions
it has evolved to serve. This is what he means by language
as social semiotic (see Chapter 1, pages 13–15).*

The particular form taken by the grammatical system of language
is closely related to the social and personal needs that language is
required to serve. But in order to bring this out it is necessary to
look at both the system of language and its functions at the same
time; otherwise we will lack any theoretical basis for generaliza-
tions about how language is used. ...

It is fairly obvious that language is used to serve a variety of different needs, but until we examine its grammar there is no clear
reason for classifying its uses in any particular way. However,
when we examine the meaning potential of language itself, we
find that the vast numbers of options embodied in it combine into
a very few relatively independent 'networks'; and these networks
of options correspond to certain basic functions of language. This
enables us to give an account of the different functions of language that is relevant to the general understanding of linguistic
structure rather than to any particular psychological or sociological investigation.

▷ *What is the relationship between the networks of options in
the grammar and the basic functions of language?*

1. Language serves for the expression of 'content': that is, of the
speaker's experience of the real world, including the inner
world of his own consciousness. We may call this the
ideational function ... In serving this function, language also

gives structure to experience, and helps to determine our way of looking at things, so that it requires some intellectual effort to see them in any other way than that which our language suggests to us.

2. Language serves to establish and maintain social relations: for the expression of social roles, which include the communication roles created by language itself—for example the roles of questioner or respondent, which we take on by asking or answering a question; and also for getting things done, by means of the interaction between one person and another. Through this function, which we may refer to as *interpersonal*, social groups are delimited, and the individual is identified and reinforced, since by enabling him to interact with others' language also serves in the expression and development of his own personality. ...

3. Finally, language has to provide for making links with itself and with features of the situation in which it is used. We may call this the *textual* function, since this is what enables the speaker or writer to construct 'texts', or connected passages of discourse that is situationally relevant; and enables the listener or reader to distinguish a text from a random set of sentences.

▷ The ideational function of language 'gives structure to experience'. What do you think Halliday means by saying that this 'helps to determine our way of looking at things'?

▷ How do you think it is possible for social roles to be 'created by language itself'?

▷ How do you see the textual function as relating to the other two?

Text 7

M.A.K.HALLIDAY: *Language as Social Semiotic.*
Edward Arnold 1978, pages 16–17

This text and the one which follows are both concerned with how concepts of the nature of language, as outlined in Texts 5 and 6, relate to the conditions for its acquisition. If you take an innate or 'nativist' view, then the child is already genetically

provided with a language organ which only needs the environ-
ment to stimulate growth. If you take an 'environmentalist'
position, there is no such organ, but only a general cognitive
capability which interacts with environmental factors to yield
different languages. In the 'nativist' view, of which Chomsky
is a proponent, the common properties of language in general
already exist before different languages are formed. In the
'environmentalist' view, which Halliday adopts, the common
properties of language emerge because different languages are
all subject to the same kinds of environmental influence (see
Chapter 1, pages 11–15).

In the psychological sphere, there have recently been two alternative lines of approach to the question of language development.
These have been referred to as the 'nativist' and the 'environmentalist' positions. Everyone agrees, of course, that human beings
are biologically endowed with the ability to learn language, and
that this is a uniquely human attribute—no other species has it,
however much a chimpanzee or a dolphin may be trained to operate with words or symbols. But the nativist view holds that there
is a specific language-learning faculty, distinct from other learning
faculties, and that this provides the human infant with a ready-
made and rather detailed blueprint of the structure of language.
Learning his mother tongue consists in fitting the patterns of
whatever language he hears around him into the framework
which he already possesses. The environmentalist view considers
that language learning is not fundamentally distinct from other
kinds of learning; it depends on those same mental faculties that
are involved in all aspects of the child's learning processes. Rather
than having built into his genetic makeup a set of concrete universals of language, what the child has is the ability to process certain
highly abstract types of cognitive relation which underlie (among
other things) the linguistic system; the very specific properties of
language are not innate, and therefore the child is more dependent on his environment—on the language he hears around him,
together with the contexts in which it is uttered—for the success-
ful learning of his mother tongue. In a sense, therefore, the difference of views is a recurrence of the old controversy of nature and
nurture, or heredity and environment, in a new guise.

▷ *Halliday says in this text that humans are 'biologically endowed with the ability to learn language'. Chomsky, in Text 5, says that humans are 'specifically designed' to learn language. So do their views differ?*

▷ *According to this text, how might the child's language learning ability be related to heredity and/or environment?*

Text 8

NOAM CHOMSKY: *Rules and Representations.*
Blackwell 1980, pages 44–5

It seems reasonable to assume that the language faculty—and, I would guess, other mental organs—develops in the individual along an intrinsically determined course under the triggering effect of appropriate social interaction and partially shaped by the environment—English is not Japanese, just as the distribution of horizontal and vertical receptors in the visual cortex can be modified by early visual experience. The environment provides the information that questions are formed by the movement of a question word and that 'each other' is a reciprocal expression; in other languages this is not the case, so that these cannot be properties of biological endowment in specific detail. Beyond such information, much of our knowledge reflects our modes of cognition, and is therefore not limited to inductive generalization from experience, let alone any training that we may have received. And just as the visual system of a cat, though modified by experience, will never be that of a bee or a frog, so the human language faculty will develop only one of the human languages, a narrowly constrained set.

▷ *In this text, Chomsky says that the features of particular languages (like the way questions are formed in English) 'cannot be properties of biological endowment in specific detail'. In Text 7, Halliday says: 'the very specific properties of language are not innate'. Are they saying the same thing?*

▷ *In this text and Text 7, reference is made to the influence of the environment. Is the influence seen as the same in each case?*

Chapter 2
The scope of linguistics

Text 9

FERDINAND DE SAUSSURE: *Course in General Linguistics*
(edited by Charles Bally and Albert Sechehaye, and translated
by Wade Baskin). Philosophical Library 1959, pages 13–14

*Saussure is generally regarded as one of the principal founders
of modern linguistics. This text is taken from his celebrated*
Cours de Linguistique Générale. *This work, based on
Saussure's lectures and published posthumously, was not of
his own composition, but compiled from the notes of his students and subsequently translated. Here, we find the distinction between* langue *and* parole, *and the identification of*
langue, *the idealized common social knowledge of language,
as the proper concern of linguistics as a discipline (see Chapter
2, pages 21–4).*

... If we could embrace the sum of word-images stored in the
minds of all individuals, we could identify the social bond that
constitutes language [*langue*]. It is a storehouse filled by the members of a given community through their active use of speaking
[*parole*], a grammatical system that has a potential existence in
each brain, or, more specifically, in the brains of a group of
individuals. For language [*langue*] is not complete in any speaker;
it exists perfectly only within a collectivity.

In separating language [*langue*] from speaking [*parole*] we are
at the same time separating: (1) what is social from what is individual; and (2) what is essential from what is accessory and more
or less accidental.

Language [*langue*] is not a function of the speaker; it is a product that is passively assimilated by the individual. It never requires
premeditation, and reflection enters in only for the purpose of
classification ...

Speaking [*parole*], on the contrary, is an individual act. It is wil-
ful and intellectual. Within the act, we should distinguish between:
(1) the combinations by which the speaker uses the language code
for expressing his own thought; and (2) the psychophysical mechanism that allows him to exteriorize those combinations.

▷ *What do you think Saussure means by saying that 'language is not complete in any speaker, it exists perfectly only within a collectivity'?*

▷ *The terms 'system', 'potential', and 'social' are all used in this text to define* langue. *The same terms are used in Texts 6 and 7 to describe language as social semiotic. Are they used in the same way? Would you conclude that Saussure's view of language is the same as Halliday's?*

Text 10

NOAM CHOMSKY: *Aspects of the Theory of Syntax.*
MIT Press 1965, pages 3–4

Some fifty years after Saussure first introduced his distinction between langue *and* parole, *Chomsky, following the same principles of idealization, proposed a similar distinction between competence and performance (see Chapter 2, pages 24–7). This, too, identifies abstract knowledge of language as the concern of linguistics, dissociated from the particular features of actual language behaviour. So linguistics in this view has to do with the ideal rather than the real.*

Linguistic theory is concerned primarily with an ideal speaker–listener, in a completely homogeneous speech-community, who knows its language perfectly and is unaffected by such grammatically irrelevant conditions as memory limitations, distractions, shifts of attention and interest, and errors (random or characteristic) in applying his knowledge of the language in actual performance. This seems to me to have been the position of the founders of modern general linguistics, and no cogent reason for modifying it has been offered. To study actual linguistic performance, we must consider the interaction of a variety of factors, of which the underlying competence of the speaker–hearer is only one. In this respect, study of language is no different from empirical investigation of other complex phenomena.

▷ *What other factors do you think need to be considered apart from competence in the study of actual performance?*

▷ *In actuality, of course, there is no such thing as an ideal speaker–listener or a homogeneous speech community. So why is this not a 'cogent reason for modifying' the position of modern linguistics that Chomsky accepts?*

We thus make a fundamental distinction between *competence* (the speaker–hearer's knowledge of his language) and *performance* (the actual use of language in concrete situations). Only under the idealization set forth in the preceding paragraph is performance a direct reflection of competence. In actual fact, it obviously could not directly reflect competence. A record of natural speech will show numerous false starts, deviations from rules, changes of plan in mid-course, and so on. The problem for the linguist, as well as for the child learning the language, is to determine from the data of performance the underlying system of rules that has been mastered by the speaker–hearer and that he puts to use in actual performance. Hence, in the technical sense, linguistic theory is mentalistic, since it is concerned with discovering a mental reality underlying actual behavior. Observed use of language or hypothesized dispositions to respond, habits, and so on, may provide evidence as to the nature of this mental reality, but surely cannot constitute the actual subject matter of linguistics, if this is to be a serious discipline. The distinction I am noting here is related to the *langue–parole* distinction of Saussure; but it is necessary to reject his concept of *langue* as merely a systematic inventory of items and to return rather to the Humboldtian conception of underlying competence as a system of generative processes. ...

A grammar of a language purports to be a description of the ideal speaker–hearer's intrinsic competence. If the grammar is, furthermore, perfectly explicit—in other words, if it does not rely on the intelligence of the understanding reader but rather provides an explicit analysis of his contribution—we may (somewhat redundantly) call it a *generative grammar*.

▷ *Performance in 'natural speech' is not a direct reflection of competence because of false starts, etc. But what of written performance? Is this a direct reflection of competence? If not, why not?*

▷ *How is the competence–performance distinction related to that between* langue–parole? *And what do you think is the difference between 'a systematic inventory of items' and 'a system of generative processes'?*

ROY HARRIS: 'Redefining linguistics' in Hayley G. Davis and
Talbot J. Taylor (eds.): *Redefining Linguistics*. Routledge
1990, pages 37–8

*The idealized model of language proposed by Saussure and
Chomsky as a theoretical pre-requisite for linguistic enquiry is
not a universally accepted orthodoxy, as the next two texts
make clear. The first text questions its theoretical validity. The
term 'ideal' is in itself ambiguous: it can mean an abstract
model, but it can also mean a stereotype of excellence (for
example, 'an ideal husband') and this is a source of confusion.*

The fixed code and the homogeneous speech community, it is
claimed, are merely theoretical idealizations, which it is necessary
for linguistics to adopt, just as other sciences adopt for theoretical
purposes idealizations which do not correspond to the observable
facts. Thus, for example, geometry postulates such idealizations
as perfectly parallel lines and points with no dimensions; but
these are not to be found in the world of visible, measurable
objects. Nevertheless it would be a mistake to protest on this
ground that the theoretical foundations of geometry are inadequate or unsound. Analogously, it is held, idealizations of the
kind represented by the fixed code are not only theoretically legitimate but theoretically essential in linguistics; and those who
object to them simply fail to understand the role of idealization in
scientific inquiry.

Unfortunately, this defence of the orthodox doctrine is based
on a false comparison. Broadly speaking, two different types of
intellectual idealization may be distinguished. In the exact sciences, and also in applied sciences such as architecture and eco-
nomics, idealizations play an important role in processes of
calculation. Any such idealization which was in practice dis-
covered to be misleading or ineffectual when put to the test by
being used as a basis for calculation would very soon be aban-
doned. In the humanities, by contrast, idealization plays an
entirely different role. The ideal monarch, the ideal state, and the
ideal mother are abstractions not set up in order to be used as a
basis for calculation, but as prescriptive stereotypes on which to
focus the discussion of controversial issues concerning how

human beings should conduct themselves and how human affairs should be managed. But the ideal speech community, the ideal language, and the ideal speaker–hearer turn out to be neither one thing nor the other. They are neither abstractions to which items and processes in the real world may be regarded as approximating for purposes of calculation; nor are they models held up for purposes of exemplification or emulation. In fact they are, more mundanely, steps in a process of explanation; and as such subject to all the usual criticisms which explanatory moves incur (including, for instance, that they fail to explain what they purport to explain).

What is particularly damning in the case of orthodox linguistics is that its idealized account of speech communication not merely fails to give a verifiable explanation of what passes for speech communication in the world of every day, but actually makes it theoretically impossible for a linguist proceeding on the basis of this idealization to come up with any linguistic analysis at all.

▷ *In Text 10, Chomsky presents the orthodox doctrine that is criticized in this text, and says that 'no cogent reason has been offered for modifying it'. Do you think this text provides such a cogent reason?*

▷ *What reasons are there for saying that this idealization makes it 'theoretically impossible' to do 'any linguistic analysis at all'?*

Text 12

D.H.HYMES: 'On communicative competence' in J. B. Pride and J. Holmes (eds.): *Sociolinguistics*. Penguin 1972, pages 278–9, 281

In this text, the objection to the orthodox idealization of language for linguistics is based on the observation that language is much more than an abstract system of rules for linking form and meaning: it is also the use of such rules to communicate (see Chapter 2, pages 27–8). A valid model of language should therefore also account for its use in 'communicative conduct and social life'.

We break irrevocably with the model that restricts the design of language to one face toward referential meaning, one toward sound, and that defines the organization of language as solely consisting of rules for linking the two. Such a model implies naming to be the sole use of speech, as if languages were never organized to lament, rejoice, beseech, admonish, aphorize, inveigh ... , for the many varied forms of persuasion, direction, expression and symbolic play. A model of language must design it with a face toward communicative conduct and social life.

Attention to the social dimension is thus not restricted to occasions on which social factors seem to interfere with or restrict the grammatical. The engagement of language in social life has a positive, productive aspect. There are rules of use without which the rules of grammar would be useless. Just as rules of syntax can control aspects of phonology, and just as semantic rules perhaps control aspects of syntax, so rules of speech acts enter as a controlling factor for linguistic form as a whole. ...

The acquisition of competence for use, indeed, can be stated in the same terms as acquisition of competence for grammar. Within the developmental matrix in which knowledge of the sentences of a language is acquired, children also acquire knowledge of a set of ways in which sentences are used. From a finite experience of speech acts and their interdependence with sociocultural features, they develop a general theory of the speaking appropriate in their community, which they employ, like other forms of tacit cultural knowledge (competence) in conducting and interpreting social life ...

There are several sectors of communicative competence, of which the grammatical is one. Put otherwise, there is behavior, and, underlying it, there are several systems of rules reflected in the judgements and abilities of those whose messages the behavior manifests.

▷ *'There are rules of use without which the rules of grammar would be useless.' What do you think Hymes has in mind here? Can you think of examples of such 'rules of use'?*

▷ *How far do the views expressed here and those expressed in Texts 8 and 10 illustrate the 'two alternative lines of approach to the question of language development' referred to by Halliday in Text 7?*

▷ *Halliday, in Text 6, talks about 'functions of language' and*

Hymes, in this text, talks about 'rules of use' and 'rules of speech acts'. Do you think that the three expressions mean much the same thing?

Text 13
M.ATKINSON, D.KILBY, and I.ROCA: *Foundations of General Linguistics* (2nd edn.) Unwin Hyman 1988, pages 42–3

Hymes's objection to the orthodox idealization of language, and his proposal to extend the concept of competence to include communicative use as well as linguistic knowledge, have themselves come under attack. One can agree that communication is a matter of interest, and concede that the orthodox concept of linguistic competence does not account for it, just as one can concede that the engine is not the whole car. But so what?

Whether any sense can be attached to Hymes's own notion of communicative competence is not something we shall discuss here, but two things seem to be clear. In the same way that it makes sense to talk about a sentence being well-formed, ambiguous, etc., it also makes sense to talk about a sentence being *appropriate* to encode a particular message under certain circumstances; and, in the same way that it makes sense to talk about a native speaker's knowledge in connection with well-formedness, ambiguity, etc., it is also intelligible to talk about appropriateness in similar terms. Thus, it appears to be correct that if it is the whole gamut of conversational and communicative behaviour in which we are interested, there is more to it than mere linguistic competence. But what follows from this? A realisation that the engine is not the only part vital to the functioning of the car does not lead us to reject it as a part, nor does it lead us to insist that those people who focus their attention exclusively on engines should switch their interests to cars–as–a–whole. It might, of course, be the case that our understanding of engines will be enriched by studying cars–as–a–whole just as it might be the case that our understanding of language-structure will be enriched by studying communication–as–a–whole ... but this is not self-evidently true and both strategies must be extensively explored in order for the protagonists to have any leverage.

▷ Do you find this analogy convincing? Is it actually the case that car engines can be studied without regard to the functioning of the car?

▷ On the evidence of Text 6, how do you suppose Halliday might respond to the idea that language structure can be understood in dissociation from communication?

▷ On the evidence of Text 12, does Hymes in fact reject linguistic competence (the engine) as part of communicative competence (the car-as-a-whole)? And does he in fact insist that those whose focus of interest is on language structure should shift their attention to communication?

Chapter 3
Principles and levels of analysis

Text 14
DAVID CRYSTAL: *Linguistics* (2nd edn.) Penguin 1985, pages 73–4

To classify things into categories is to identify features of sameness, and to disregard any differences as irrelevant to your purpose (see Chapter 3, pages 30–2). Since linguistic signs are combinations of form and meaning, we might classify them in reference to one or the other. The traditional way of classifying signs as 'parts of speech' (noun, verb, adjective, adverb, and so on) was to focus on meaning. This has its problems. An alternative is to consider how the forms function as components in larger structures (see Chapter 3, pages 32–5). But this may have its problems too.

In order to present an alternative approach, the linguist must first thoroughly understand the inadequacies of the approaches already available, and sometimes these are very explicit. One illustration of this is the vagueness of definition which surrounds many of the central categories of the older models. The parts of speech, for instance, are sometimes defined in a very unhelpful way. These categories were set up in order to explain how the grammar of a language 'worked'; but many of the definitions seemed to have nothing to do with grammar. A standard example is the noun, regularly defined as 'the name of a person, place or thing'. But this definition tells us nothing about the *grammar* of nouns at all; it merely gives us a rather vague indication of what nouns are used to refer to in the outside world (which is part of what we mean by the 'meaning' of nouns). A grammatical definition of noun ought to provide grammatical information—information about their function in a sentence, about their inflectional characteristics, and so on. The above definition gives us none of this. Moreover, the information which it does give, apart from its irrelevance, is so inexplicit as to be almost useless. Are abstract nouns like 'beauty' included in this definition? If so, under what heading? Can we reasonably say that 'beauty' is a 'thing'? And what about those nouns which refer to actions (supposedly, in traditional grammar, a feature of verbs), such as *kick* (as in *I gave him a kick*)? Metaphysical questions of this kind are surely not the province of grammarians, and they ought to steer well clear of them.

▷ *The writer says that the definition of a noun based on meaning is 'so inexplicit as to be almost useless'. But he defines 'beauty' as a member of a category of abstract nouns. Is there any inconsistency here?*

▷ *The argument in this text is that grammatical information can be entirely dissociated from meaning. How consistent is this with the views expressed in Texts 6 and 12? Would Halliday and Hymes accept that 'what nouns are used to refer to in the outside world' is irrelevant information as far as grammar is concerned?*

Text 15

R.H.ROBINS: *General Linguistics: An Introductory Survey* (4th edn.) Longman 1989, pages 44–6

The standard way of classifying linguistic forms is to establish how they relate to each other as components or constituents of larger structures. This involves locating them on two dimensions: the horizontal one which shows how a form (X) combines with others (W+X+Y) in a syntagmatic relationship, and the vertical one which shows how otherwise different froms (Xa, Xb, Xc) can function in the same place in structure in a paradigmatic relationship (see Chapter 3, pages 32–5).

The next two texts provide further discussion of these dimensions of analysis.

It is a commonplace today to say that linguistics is STRUCTURAL, and that languages, as analysed by linguists, are treated STRUCTURALLY. This is a statement about the elements (constants) set up by abstraction in the description and analysis of languages. These are considered and treated as being related to one another by their very nature and so forming interrelated systems rather than mere aggregates of individuals. A metaphor may clarify this distinction. The members of an orchestra are all related to each other by their specific roles as orchestral players therein, both within smaller groups and in the whole orchestra (*eg* member of the woodwind section, first fiddle among the strings, and so on). Each performs his function by virtue of his place in relation to the others, and players cannot be added to or taken away from an orchestra without altering its essential musical quality and potentialities. On the other hand the audience at a concert is more like a simple aggregate; ten more members or five fewer, be they men or women and wherever they may choose to sit, make no difference to the whole audience in its capacity as an audience.

At each level the formal constituents of the analysis, the elements abstracted, are established and defined as parts thereof by their relations with other constituents at the same level. ...

Essentially the relations between linguistic elements are of two kinds of dimensions, usually designated syntagmatic and paradigmatic. SYNTAGMATIC relations are those holding between elements forming serial structures, or 'strings' as they are sometimes called, at a given level, referable to, though of course not identical with, the temporal flow of utterance or linear stretches of writing. [For example] the word sequence *take* and *care*, the transcription /'teɪk/ 'keə/, the more abstract phonological representation CVVC CVV (C = consonantal element, V = vocalic element), and the grammatical arrangement verb + noun are all, at different levels, structures of syntagmatically related components. By reason of their referability to the actual material of the spoken (or written) utterance, syntagmatic relations may be considered the primary dimension. PARADIGMATIC relations are those holding between comparable elements at particular places in structures, *eg*

initial consonant	*take*	/teɪk/
	m	/m/
	b	/b/
postverbal noun	*take*	*care*
		pains
		thought
		counsel

and more generally between the comparable elements of structures in classes (*eg* consonants, verbs), or in the language as a whole (*eg* phonemes (phonological elements), word classes ('part of speech')).

Structure and *system*, and their derivatives, are often used almost interchangeably, but it is useful to employ *structure*, as in the preceding paragraph, specifically with reference to groupings of syntagmatically related elements, and *system* with reference to classes of paradigmatically related elements.

▷ *Why does the writer suggest that 'syntagmatic relations may be considered the primary dimension'?*

▷ *Serial structures, or 'strings' of elements are said to be 're-ferable to, though of course not identical with, the temporal flow of utterance or linear stretches of writing'. Why 'of course not identical'?*

▷ *Paradigmatic relations are said to hold 'between comparable elements'. What makes elements comparable?*

Text 16

JOHN LYONS: *Introduction to Theoretical Linguistics.* Cambridge University Press 1968, pages 73–4

This text provides further discussion on the dimensions of linguistic analysis, on syntagmatic and paradigmatic relations.

By virtue of its potentiality of occurrence in a certain context a linguistic unit enters into relations of two different kinds. It enters into *paradigmatic* relations with all the units which can also occur in the same context (whether they contrast or are in free variation with the unit in question); and it enters into *syntagmatic* relations with the other units of the same level with which it occurs and which constitute its context. [For example] by virtue of its potentiality of occurrence in the context /-et/ the expression-element /b/ stands in paradigmatic relationship with /p/, /s/, etc.; and in syntagmatic relationship with /e/ and /t/. Likewise, /e/ is in paradigmatic relationship with /ɪ/, /æ/, etc., and in syntagmatic relationship with /b/ and /t/. And /t/ is related paradigmatically with /d/, /n/, etc., and syntagmatically with /b/ and /e/.

Paradigmatic and syntagmatic relationships are also relevant at the word-level, and indeed at every level of linguistic description. For example, by virtue of its potentiality of occurrence in such contexts as *a ... of milk*, the word *pint* contracts paradigmatic relations with such other words as *bottle, cup, gallon,* etc., and syntagmatic relations with *a, of* and *milk*. In fact, words (and other grammatical units) enter into paradigmatic and syntagmatic relations of various kinds. 'Potentiality of occurrence' can be interpreted with or without regard to the question whether the resultant phrase or sentence is meaningful; with or without regard to the situations in which actual utterances are produced; with or without regard to the dependencies that hold between different sentences in connected discourse; and so on. ... it must be emphasized that all linguistic units contract syntagmatic and paradigmatic relations with other units of the same level (expression-elements with expression-elements, words with words, etc.); that the *context* of a linguistic unit is specifiable in terms of its syntagmatic relations; and that the range of contexts in which it is said to occur, as well as the extent of the class of units with which it is said to be paradigmatically related, will depend upon the interpretation explicitly or implicitly attached to 'potentiality of occurrence' (or 'acceptability').

▷ *Reference is made in Text 15 to 'comparable elements at particular places in structures'. Does this mean the same as 'units which can occur in the same context' or which have the same 'potentiality of occurrence'?*

▷ *In Text 16, the author talks of the paradigmatic dimension as covering 'many different types of contrast, according to the different criteria employed'. In this text, the writer talks of the identification of paradigmatic relations as dependent upon the interpretation explicitly or implicitly attached to 'potentiality of occurrence'. Are they making the same point?*

▷ *Consider the nonsense rhyme:*

'Twas brillig and the slithy toves
Did gyre and gimble in the wabe. (see Chapter 5, page 54)

What syntagmatic and paradigmatic relations can you iden-
tify and at what levels? And how does this exercise illustrate
the point that the identification of paradigmatic relations
depends on how the notion 'potentiality of occurrence' is
interpreted?

Chapters 4 and 5
Areas of enquiry: focus on form and meaning

Text 17
FRANK PALMER: *Grammar* (2nd edn.) Penguin 1984,
pages 34–5

This text takes up the issue of classification discussed in Text
14. It is standard practice in linguistics to make clear de-
marcations between different areas of enquiry, so that the
criteria for making grammatical distinctions between forms,
for example, have to be independent of what these forms
might mean semantically. The difficulty about this is that cer-
tain categories, like number (singular and plural), seem to
belong to both grammar and semantics. So can grammar be
divorced from semantics so completely?

Another of the misconceptions that we discussed is that grammar
is essentially concerned with meaning. In linguistics, however, we
draw a distinction between grammar and semantics (the study of
meaning) and insist that they are not identified.

It is easy enough to show that grammatical distinctions are not
semantic ones by indicating the many cases where there is not a
one-to-one correspondence. An often quoted example is that of
oats and *wheat*. The former is clearly plural and the latter singular.
This is partly indicated by the ending –*s* (though this is not an
unambiguous sign of the plural in view of a word like *news* which
is singular) but it is clearly shown by the fact that we say *The oats*
are …, The wheat is … . We cannot, however, say in all seriousness
that *oats* are 'more than one' while *wheat* is 'one', the traditional

definitions of singular and plural. Some people might say that this is true of English at least, but that is only to say that *oats* is grammatically plural and *wheat* grammatically singular. If these people go on to insist that the English think of *oats* as plural and of *wheat* as singular, then this has to be rejected as simply false. Further examples are to be found in *foliage* vs *leaves*, in English *hair* which is singular vs French *cheveux*, plural. These distinctions are grammatical and do not directly correspond to any categories of meaning.

▷ *The idea that the English think of 'oats' as plural and 'wheat' as singular 'has to be rejected as simply false'. On what grounds, do you think, does such an idea have to be rejected as false? Do you think the same could be said of 'foliage' and 'leaves'?*

▷ *So-called collective nouns in English, like 'team', 'committee', and 'family' are singular in form but can function with plural verbs (for example, 'The team are confident that they will win.') What bearing does this have on the argument here?*

▷ *The writer of this text asserts that it is a misconception that 'grammar is essentially concerned with meaning'. On the evidence of Text 6, do you think Halliday would agree with this absolute distinction between grammar and semantics?*

Text 18

P. H. MATTHEWS: *Morphology* (2nd edn.), in the series 'Cambridge Textbooks in Linguistics'. Cambridge University Press 1991, pages 2–3

Whereas Text 17 drew a dividing line between grammar and semantics, this text ranges over the whole area of linguistic study and indicates the boundaries of the different 'subfields' of phonology, phonetics, syntax, semantics, pragmatics, and morphology. The boundaries seem to be drawn somewhat differently here. And they do not seem to be so clear cut.

In describing a language all four varying facets—sounds, constructions, meanings and forms of words—have to be given due attention.

In the same spirit, the field of linguistic theory may be said to include at least four major subfields. The first is concerned with the study of speech sounds, a subject which in modern structural linguistics is handled on two theoretical levels. Of these the level of phonology is concerned with the functioning of sound-units within the systems of individual languages, whereas that of phonetics is concerned with the nature and typology of speech sounds in themselves. The second major subfield is that of syntax (from a Greek word meaning a 'putting together' or 'arranging' of elements), which traditionally covers both the constructions of phrases and sentences and also features of meaning which are associated with them. For example, the Interrogative (Has he sold the gong?) is different both in construction and in meaning from the Non-interrogative or Declarative (He has sold the gong). The third subfield of semantics then reduces to the study of word meanings—to which perhaps we may add the meanings of idioms ... or of special phrases generally. Traditionally the problems of semantics have often been assigned to the dictionary. However, the oppositions of word meanings also lend themselves to structural analysis, most notably in specific 'semantic fields' such as those of kinship, colour terms, occupations, types of skill and knowledge and so on. In addition, the limits of syntax and semantics have frequently been disputed both within and between the various structural schools. According to some, constructional meanings would also belong to semantics—syntax being reduced to the formal distribution of words and groups of words. Other writers make a further distinction between semantics, as a study of the meanings of words and sentences in the abstract, and pragmatics, as that of sentences used in specific situations. According to others, syntax itself is partly a matter of word meanings: for example, it is implicit in the meaning of 'to sell' or 'to hit' that it can take an Object. On many such issues, the debate continues in full vigour.

The last major subfield is that of morphology ... that branch of linguistics which is concerned with the 'forms of words' in different uses and constructions.

▷ *According to this text, in what subfields of linguistics is meaning accounted for?*

▷ Are the views expressed here of the relationship between syntax and meaning consistent with those expressed in Text 17?

▷ According to this text, the two expressions 'Has he sold the gong?' and 'He has sold the gong' are different in meaning. Are they necessarily different in meaning, and if they are not, what implications might this have for the relationship between syntax and phonology, and between syntax, semantics, and pragmatics?

Text 19

N. V. SMITH: *The Twitter Machine: Reflections on Language.* Blackwell 1989, pages 5–6

The writer of this text defines different areas of linguistic enquiry by reference to the kinds of information we need to have as components of our knowledge of language, or, as he puts it, as modules of grammar. So if we take a word from the lexicon (our knowledge of vocabulary) we can deal with it by reference to the rules of phonology, syntax, semantics, and so on. The word also provides access to non-linguistic knowledge.

If our knowledge of language is correctly viewed as being in the form of rules, a core part of linguistics will be to specify the types and properties of these rules. As a minimum we need to distinguish *lexical, syntactic, semantic, phonological* and *morphological* information, each of which is said to constitute a *component* or (sub-module) of the grammar. That is, just as language is one module of the mind, syntax is one module of the grammar, and within syntax there are further modules, each characterized by particular principles and properties.

The *lexicon*, representing our knowledge of the vocabulary of our language, contains information relating to each of the four other components about every word in the individual's language. For instance, *bumblebee* is a noun (syntactic information), is stressed on the first syllable (phonological information), means a kind of insect (semantic information), and is composed of two sub-parts, *bumble* and *bee*, (morphological information). The lexicon also serves as a means of access to our non-linguistic knowledge, containing information of an *encyclopaedic* kind: for example, that bumblebees are hairy, buzz, sting when offended, fall into two main genera, *Bombus* and *Psythirus*, and are spelt 'b–u–m–b–l–e–b–e–e'. Whereas the linguistic knowledge we have is likely to be essentially invariant from speaker to speaker, our encyclopaedic knowledge is much more idiosyncratic: I am very fond of bumblebees and associate them with heather and holidays; someone with a bee sting allergy is likely to have a different view.

▷ *What does the term 'grammar' cover in this text? Is it being used here in the same sense as in Text 17?*

▷ *How far do you think the 'modules of grammar' here correspond with the 'subfields' of linguistic theory outlined in Text 18?*

▷ *What do you think is the difference between linguistic and encyclopaedic knowledge? Do you think that the spelling of a word is a matter of encyclopaedic knowledge? Do you agree with the assertion that linguistic knowledge 'is likely to be essentially invariant from speaker to speaker'?*

Text 20

J.R.SEARLE: *Speech Acts.* Cambridge University Press 1969, pages 17–18

Texts 20 and 21 deal with the relationship between the speech act, the sentence, and the utterance, and therefore with the distinction between semantics and pragmatics (see Chapter 5, pages 61–5). In this text, Searle argues that the study of the meanings of speech acts is not essentially different from the study of sentence meaning, and is therefore part of semantics. And yet the meaning of a speech act is dependent too on its being performed in an appropriate (non-linguistic) context.

There are, therefore, not two irreducibly distinct semantic studies, one a study of the meanings of sentences and one a study of the performances of speech acts. For just as it is part of our notion of the meaning of a sentence that a literal utterance of that sentence with that meaning in a certain context would be the performance of a particular speech act, so it is part of our notion of a speech act that there is a possible sentence (or sentences) the utterance of which in a certain context would in virtue of its (or their) meaning constitute a performance of that speech act.

The speech act or acts performed in the utterance of a sentence are in general a function of the meaning of the sentence. The meaning of a sentence does not in all cases uniquely determine what speech act is performed in a given utterance of that sentence, for a speaker may mean more than what he actually says, but it is always in principle possible for him to say exactly what he means. Therefore, it is in principle possible for every speech act one performs or could perform to be uniquely determined by a given sentence (or set of sentences), given the assumptions that the speaker is speaking literally and that the context is appropriate. And for these reasons a study of the meaning of sentences is not in principle distinct from a study of speech acts. Properly construed, they are the same study. Since every meaningful sentence in virtue of its meaning can be used to perform a particular speech act (or range of speech acts), and since every possible speech act can in principle be given an exact formulation in a sentence or sentences (assuming an appropriate context of utterance), the study of the meanings of sentences and the study of speech acts are not two independent studies but one study from two different points of view.

▷ *Speech acts are referred to by Hymes in Text 12, where he associates them with rules of use. Is this consistent with the view of speech acts expressed by Searle in this text?*

▷ *The writer says that sentence meaning can uniquely determine speech act meaning given an appropriate context. In reference to Text 19, what kind of information would we need to establish the appropriateness of such contextual conditions? And, in reference to Text 18, would this fall within the scope of semantics or pragmatics?*

Text 21
DIANE BLAKEMORE: *Understanding Utterances: An Introduction to Pragmatics*. Blackwell 1992, pages 39–40

The writer here draws a clear distinction between semantics and pragmatics, and, in respect to the latter, acknowledges the relevance of non-linguistic knowledge (which would include the knowledge of appropriate contexts for speech acts) in the interpretation of utterances. An utterance can be acceptable (that is to say, appropriate in context) without being grammatically well-formed as a sentence. This would seem to suggest that speech-act meaning cannot, after all, be subsumed under the study of sentence meaning.

Since an utterance consists of a certain sequence or phrase with a certain syntactic structure and made up of words with certain meanings, its interpretation will depend on the hearer's linguistic knowledge. However, since it is produced by a particular speaker on a particular occasion and the hearer's task is to discover what that speaker meant on that occasion, its interpretation will also depend on the non-linguistic knowledge that she brings to bear. ...

The assumption ... is that there is a distinction between a hearer's knowledge of her language and her knowledge of the world. In this section I shall argue that it is this distinction that underlies the distinction between *semantics* and *pragmatics*. ...

The assumption that there is a distinction between linguistic and non-linguistic knowledge marks our approach as *modular*, and thus as consistent with the view of language found in Chomskyan generative grammar. According to this approach, knowledge of language is one of a system of interacting modules which make up the mind, each of which has its own particular properties. This implies that the mind does not develop as a whole, but with specific capacities developing in their own ways and in their own time. In other words, knowledge of language cannot be regarded as the result of general intelligence. It also implies that actual linguistic performance—that is, the way we use language—is a result of the interaction of a number of different systems, and that the acceptability of an utterance may be affected by factors other than its grammatical well-formedness. An utterance may consist of a perfectly grammatical sentence and still be unacceptable. Equally, an ungrammatical sentence may be used in the production of a perfectly acceptable utterance.

▷ *How do the last two sentences in this text key in with the points made in Text 12?*

▷ *How do the points made about modules in this text correspond to what is said about them in Text 19?*

▷ *Reference is made here to the 'occasion' of utterance. In Text*

20 *reference is made to the 'context' of utterance. Do they mean the same, and are they given the same weight in the description of meaning?*

Chapter 6
Current issues

Text 22
DEBORAH SCHIFFRIN: *Approaches to Discourse.*
Blackwell 1994, pages 418–19

This text raises questions about the scope of linguistics as a discipline (see Chapter 6, pages 69–72). When the study of language is extended to account for the pragmatics of discourse (see Chapter 5, pages 61–8) it necessarily becomes involved in the real world contexts in which language is used for communication. This takes us beyond the scope of linguistics as traditionally conceived and into a broader interdisciplinary enquiry about human knowledge and behaviour. Linguistics may be necessary, but it is not sufficient.

... I want to suggest that discourse cannot be analyzed—even if one considers one's analysis linguistically motivated and linguistically relevant—through one discipline alone. Consider the issues about which all discourse analysts make assumptions: structure and function, text and context, discourse and communication. In each pair of concepts, the first member is the one that fits most comfortably into the realm of linguistic inquiry. To be specific: structures can be identified at many levels of linguistic organization (sounds, sentences), but functions are usually seen as non-linguistic (e.g. cognitive, social); texts are linguistic, but contexts include non-linguistic situations and people; even discourse, although rarely seen as confined to language *per se*, is certainly more language-centred a concept than communication (which involves people, intentions, and knowledge).

In a sense, then, the need to combine the study of structure with that of function, to understand the relationship between text and context, and to make clear how discourse is related to communication, is actually a single need. This need bears directly on the interdisciplinary basis of discourse analysis. I have said that it is difficult to always know how to separate (and relate) structure and function, text and context, discourse and communication. But what I am really saying is that it is difficult to separate language from the rest of the world. It is this ultimate inability to separate language from how it is used in the world in which we live that provides the most basic reason for the interdisciplinary basis of discourse analysis. To understand the language of discourse, then, we need to understand the world in which it resides; and to understand the world in which language resides, we need to go outside of linguistics.

▷ *The writer here talks of 'the ultimate inability to separate language from how it is used in the world'. Would this necessarily invalidate the kind of idealization upon which linguistics has conventionally been based (see Chapter 2, pages 17–21, and Texts 9 and 10)?*

▷ *Reference is made in this text to 'the need to combine the study of structure with that of function'. In Text 6, Halliday says that 'it is necessary to look at both the system of language and its function at the same time'. Do you think they are making the same point?*

Text 23

JOHN SINCLAIR: *Corpus, Concordance, Collocation.*
Oxford University Press 1991, page 4

It is now possible to collect and analyse vast quantities of actually occurring language by computer. This means that observation, rather than elicitation or introspection, has become the preferred way of getting language data (see Chapter 6, pages 72–5). But the data are not the same. Corpus analysis reveals facts about usage which are not accessible to intuition. It would seem to follow that linguists' traditional dependence on their own introspection as a source of linguistic evidence must now be open to objection.

... the ability to examine large text corpora in a systematic manner allows access to a quality of evidence that has not been available before. The regularities of pattern are sometimes spectacular and, to balance [*sic*] the variation seems endless. The raw frequency of differing language events has a powerful influence on evaluation.

The comprehensive nature of simple retrieval systems is an excellent feature. No instance is overlooked, and the main features of usage are generally clear. Minor patterns remain in the background. Some very common usages are often not featured in descriptions because they are so humdrum and routine; this method brings them to the fore. Especially in lexicography, there is a marked contrast between the data collected by computer and that collected by human readers exercising their judgement on what should or should not be selected for inclusion in a dictionary.

Indeed, the contrast exposed between the impressions of language detail noted by people, and the evidence compiled objectively from texts is huge and systematic. It leads one to suppose that human intuition about language is highly specific, and not at all a good guide to what actually happens when the same people actually use the language. Students of linguistics over many years have been urged to rely heavily on their intuitions and to prefer their intuitions to actual text where there was some discrepancy. Their study has, therefore, been more about intuition than about language. It is not the purpose of this work to denigrate intuition—far from it. The way a person conceptualizes language and expresses this conceptualization is of great importance and interest precisely *because* it is not in accordance with the newly observed facts of usage.

▷ 'Indeed, the contrast exposed between the impressions of language detail noted by people, and the evidence compiled objectively from texts, is huge and systematic.' What is the textual data provided by computer analysis evidence of? Would you agree that it is indeed 'compiled objectively'?

▷ The writer here says that linguistic study which is based on the data of linguists' intuition is 'more about intuition than about language'. Do you agree? How does this view bear on the distinction between language knowledge and behaviour (see Chapter 6, pages 74–5)?

Text 24

W. LABOV: 'The judicial testing of linguistic theory' in
Deborah Tannen (ed.): *Linguistics in Context: Connecting
Observation and Understanding.* Advances in Discourse
Processes, Volume XXIX. Ablex 1988, pages 181–2

*It is not only the scope of linguistics that is currently ques-
tioned but also its role, not only its validity in theory but its
utility in practice (see Chapter 6, pages 75–7). Linguistics has
tended to be not only introspective but inward-looking too,
isolated from the real world. How can it be otherwise, given
the necessity of idealization? The writer of this text argues
that validity and utility are not distinct, that theory only has
value to the extent that it is relevant to real-life problems. This
would seem to suggest that the only valid linguistics is applied
linguistics.*

When we contrast linguistic theory with linguistic practice, we
usually conjure up a theory that builds models out of introspective judgements, extracting principles that are remote from
observation and experiment. This is not the kind of theory I have
in mind when I search for a way to establish the facts of a matter
I am involved in. ...

We are, of course, interested in theories of the greatest generality. But are these theories the end-product of linguistic activity?
Do we gather facts to serve the theory, or do we create theories to
resolve questions about the real world? I would challenge the
common understanding of our academic linguistics that we are in
the business of producing theories: that linguistic theories are our
major product. I find such a notion utterly wrong.

A sober look at the world around us shows that matters of
importance are matters of fact. There are some very large matters
of fact: the origin of the universe, the direction of continental
drift, the evolution of the human species. There are also specific
matters of fact: the innocence or guilt of a particular individual.
These are the questions to answer if we would achieve our fullest
potential as thinking beings.

General theory is useful, and the more general the theory the
more useful it is, just as any tool is more useful if it can be used for
more jobs. But it is still the application of the theory that determines

its value. A very general theory can be thought of as a missile that attains considerable altitude, and so it has much greater range than other missiles. But the value of any missile depends on whether it hits the target.

▷ Do you think that it follows that if a linguistic theory (like Chomsky's) 'builds models out of introspective judgements' it cannot enquire into matters of fact?

▷ Corpus analysis, as discussed in Text 23, deals with matters of fact on a large scale. Does this automatically give it theoretical validity?

▷ Do you agree that the value of a theory depends on how useful it is? What criteria would you use to establish its usefulness?

References

The references which follow can be classified into introductory level (marked ■□□), more advanced and consequently more technical (marked ■■□), and specialized, very demanding (marked ■■■).

Chapter 1
The nature of language

■□□

JEAN AITCHISON: *The Articulate Mammal* (3rd edn.) Routledge 1992

This book provides a very full and readable account of the experiments with primates and of the nature of human language in general.

■□□

A. AKMAJIAN, R.A. DEMERS, and R.M. HARNISH: *Linguistics: An Introduction to Language and Communication* (4th edn.) MIT Press 1995

The first part of this book (Chapters 2–5) deals in some detail with systems of animal communication and compares them with reference to three different approaches to classification, including the idea of design features. Chapter 14 describes and discusses the attempts to teach language to the two chimpanzees Washoe and Sarah.

■■■
NOAM CHOMSKY: *Reflections on Language*.
Pantheon Books 1975 (*see* Text 5)

This book originated as a series of public lectures and, though relatively non-technical, is none the less intellectually challenging. The first two chapters examine questions about the nature of language as an object of enquiry.

■□□
JOHN LYONS: *Language and Linguistics: An Introduction*.
Cambridge University Press 1981

Chapter 1 deals with aspects of human language, including design features (*see* Text 1). Chapter 8 deals with language and mind and discusses universal grammar and the notion of innateness.

■■□
RONALD WARDHAUGH: *Investigating Language: Central Problems in Linguistics*. Blackwell 1993 (*see* Text 4)

The 'problems' referred to in the title have to do with the distinctiveness of human language and mind, and language and its social use. Issues are identified and discussed in a general and non-technical way.

■□□
GEORGE YULE: *The Study of Language*.
Cambridge University Press 1985

This is an extremely accessible and well-written introduction to language, none the less authoritative for being entertaining. Chapter 3 deals with design features of human language, Chapter 4 with the chimpanzees.

Chapter 2
The scope of linguistics

■□□
E.K.BROWN: *Linguistics Today*. Fontana 1984

The book as a whole is an admirable guide to the development of generative linguistics.

Chapter 2 provides a clear account of idealization and the nature of models of linguistic description in reference to the distinctions of *langue/parole* and competence/performance.

■■■

D.H.HYMES: 'On communicative competence' in J. B. Pride and J. Holmes (eds.): *Sociolinguistics*. Penguin 1972 (*see* Text 12)

This is a much cited paper in which Hymes makes his proposal for extending the concept of competence to incorporate communicative knowledge and ability, and provides an outline scheme of what this involves.

■■□

N.SMITH and D.WILSON: *Modern Linguistics*. Penguin 1979

This is essentially an introduction to linguistics from the formalist point of view. A discussion in Chapter 1 of the nature of linguistic rules leads on, in Chapter 2, to an account of what constitutes knowledge of such rules in reference to the competence–performance distinction.

■■■

D.S.TAYLOR: 'The meaning and use of the term "competence" in linguistics and applied linguistics' in *Applied Linguistics* 9/2, 1988

This is a carefully argued investigation into the uncertainties and ambiguities in the way the term has been used.

■■■

H.G.WIDDOWSON: 'Knowledge of language and ability for use' in *Applied Linguistics* 10/2, 1989

This is a discussion of the difference between Chomsky's notion of competence and that of Hymes. The issue of *Applied Linguistics* in which the paper appears is devoted to the topic of communicative competence, and includes comments by Hymes himself.

Chapter 3
Principles and levels of analysis

■□□

DAVID CRYSTAL: *Linguistics* (2nd. edn.) Penguin 1985
(*see* Text 14)

Chapter 3 discusses the principles which define linguistics as a scientific enquiry and deals with such issues as the criteria for explicit and systematic classification of linguistic units and the objective analysis of language data. Chapter 4, 'Major themes in linguistics' takes us discursively through a whole range of different dimensions and levels of analysis.

■■□

M. DOUGLAS (ed.): *Rules and Meanings. The Anthropology of Everyday Meanings.* Penguin Books 1973

Although this is not a book on linguistics as such, it deals with principles of analysis which are just as relevant to the study of language as that of other human phenomena. It is a fascinating collection of readings about how knowledge is socially constructed and the various criteria on which classification in general is based.

■■□

JOHN LYONS: *Introduction to Theoretical Linguistics.*
Cambridge University Press 1968 (*see* Text 16)

Here (in Chapter 2) is to be found one of the surprisingly few discussions of paradigmatic–syntagmatic relations as relevant to linguistic description in general. The book as a whole provides a very detailed, and often very demanding, review of approaches to language analysis at different levels. Lyons 1981 (see above) is designed to be a less comprehensive, and less technical, version.

Chapters 4 and 5
Areas of enquiry

These areas of enquiry are included in general introductions, where, typically, they are dealt with in separate chapters.

■□□

A.AKMAJIAN, R.A.DEMERS, and R.M.HARNISH:
*Linguistics: An Introduction to Language and
Communication* (4th edn.) MIT Press 1995

Under the general heading of 'The structure of human language'
this has chapters on morphology, phonology, syntax, and semantics, in that order.

■□□

M.ATKINSON, D.KILBY, and I.ROCA: *Foundations of
General Linguistics* (2nd edn.) Unwin Hyman 1988
(*see* Text 13)

The heading here is 'Structure of language' and the sequence of
chapters is Phonetics, Phonology, Morphology, Syntax,
Semantics.

■□□

VICTORIA A. FROMKIN and ROBERT RODMAN:
An Introduction to Language (5th edn.) Harcourt Brace
Jovanovich 1993 (*see* Text 3)

The sequence of chapters is the same as in Atkinson, Kilby, and
Roca, but the areas are all included under the heading
'Grammatical aspects of language'.

These areas are given more detailed treatment in separate books:

Phonetics/Phonology

■■□

J.C.CATFORD: *A Practical Introduction to Phonetics.*
Oxford University Press 1988

This bears out the promise of its title by developing the reader's
understanding of the nature of speech sounds (mainly as segments) by providing exercises in actual performance.

■■□

J.CLARK and C.YALLOP: *An Introduction to Phonetics and
Phonology* (2nd edn.) Blackwell 1995

This provides a very comprehensive coverage of the area.
Descriptions and explanations often go into considerable detail,
but without loss of clarity.

■□□

C. DALTON and B. SEIDLHOFER: *Pronunciation,* in the series 'Language Teaching. A Scheme for Teacher Education'. Oxford University Press 1994

This book, like others in this Scheme, is designed specifically for practising teachers. Section 1 provides a clear and simple survey of phonetic and phonological aspects of the description of speech.

Morphology

■■□

F. KATAMBA: *Morphology,* in the series 'Macmillan Modern Linguistics'. The Macmillan Press 1993

This book deals with morphological theory within the framework of generative grammar, but Part 1 discusses general concepts concerning word structure and the nature of morphemes.

■■□

P. H. MATTHEWS: *Morphology* (2nd edn.), in the series 'Cambridge Textbooks in Linguistics'. Cambridge University Press 1991 (*see* Text 18)

This book does not adhere to any particular theoretical position. The early chapters take the reader through the main concepts in preparation for a discussion of more complex issues later on. It is a very well-graded guide to the subject.

Syntax

■□□

R. BATSTONE: *Grammar,* in the series 'Language Teaching. A Scheme for Teacher Education'. Oxford University Press 1994

Section 1 explains the nature of grammar, emphasizing in particular the way it functions in the expression of meaning and the key role it plays in language pedagogy.

■■■

P. H. MATTHEWS: *Syntax,* in the series 'Cambridge Textbooks in Linguistics'. Cambridge University Press 1981

This provides a clear explanation of basic concepts of syntax, like sentence construction and constituency, but also takes a critical look at a number of central theoretical issues.

■□□

FRANK PALMER: *Grammar* (2nd edn.) Penguin 1984
(*see* Text 17)

The second chapter of this book gives a clear and straightforward account of those traditional concepts of grammar which remain relevant to different approaches to description. The latter part of the book deals more specifically with generative grammar and is inevitably dated.

Semantics

■□□

JEAN AITCHISON: *Words in the Mind: An Introduction to the Mental Lexicon* (2nd edn.) Blackwell 1994

An authoritative and imaginative account of word meanings, how they figure as mental constructs and how they are accessed in use. It is both instructive and entertaining.

■□□

JOHN LYONS: *Language, Meaning, and Context*. Fontana 1981

This is a succinct and thought-provoking review of different theories of meaning, as they relate to three linguistic levels: words and phrases, sentences, and utterances beyond the sentence.

■□□

MICHAEL MCCARTHY: *Vocabulary*, in the series 'Language Teaching. A Scheme for Teacher Education'. Oxford University Press 1990

This is an introduction to the main concepts of lexical meaning and a demonstration of their relevance for language teaching.

■□□

FRANK PALMER: *Semantics* (2nd edn.) Cambridge University Press 1981

This is a brief and readable treatment of the main topics in semantics.

Pragmatics

■□□

DIANE BLAKEMORE: *Understanding Utterances: An Introduction to Pragmatics.* Blackwell 1992 (*see* Text 21)

This is a straightforward account of some of the basic issues, and provides an extensive and well-illustrated account of speech act theory and its relation to the cooperative principle.

■□□

GUY COOK: *Discourse*, in the series 'Language Teaching. A Scheme for Teacher Education'. Oxford University Press 1989

Section 1 provides a clear overview of the relevant concepts, and makes complex ideas accessible to the teachers for which the book is designed.

■□□

R.M.COULTHARD: *An Introduction to Discourse Analysis* (2nd edn.) Longman 1985

This is a readable account of certain aspects of discourse and pragmatic meaning, particularly speech acts and conversation analysis, with some indications of their relevance for language teaching and the study of literature.

■■■

STEPHEN C.LEVINSON: *Pragmatics*, in the series 'Cambridge Textbooks in Linguistics'. Cambridge University Press 1983

This is an extremely comprehensive and detailed analysis of different approaches to the study of pragmatics. The arguments are subtle, critical, and, for anybody not familiar with the field, very demanding. It is an authoritative book, but not for the novice reader.

Chapter 6
Current issues

■■■

HAYLEY G.DAVIS and TALBOT J.TAYLOR (eds.): *Redefining Linguistics.* Routledge 1990

The papers in this book, particularly that by Harris (*see* Text 11), call into question many of the fundamental formalist assumptions that have shaped linguistics since Saussure. The arguments are stimulating, if somewhat strident at times.

■■■
M.A.K.HALLIDAY: *An Introduction to Functional Grammar* (2nd edn.) Edward Arnold 1994

This book is by one of the leading proponents of a functional approach to language. The introductory chapter outlines the principles of such an approach to linguistic description.

■■□
JOHN SINCLAIR: *Corpus, Concordance, Collocation.* Oxford University Press 1991 (*see* Text 23)

An account of procedures for the computer analysis of text, and their implication for language description, by a leading pioneer in this field.

Apart from the particular works cited above, reference can also be made to the relevant entries in recent encyclopedias on linguistics:

■■■
R.E.ASHER (ed.): *The Encyclopedia of Language and Linguistics.* (12 volumes) Pergamon 1994

■■□
W.BRIGHT (ed.): *International Encyclopedia of Linguistics.* (4 volumes) Oxford University Press 1992

■□□
DAVID CRYSTAL: *The Cambridge Encyclopedia of Language.* (1 volume) Cambridge University Press 1987

■□□
KIRSTEN MALMKJAER (ed.): *The Linguistics Encyclopedia.* (1 volume) Routledge 1991

SECTION 4
Glossary

Page references to Section 1, Survey, are given at the end of each entry.

adjacency pair The term used in conversation analysis for a pair of utterances of which the first constrains the occurrence of the second, e.g. question/answer. [67]

affix A morphological element added to a word as a **bound morpheme**. *See also* **morphology**. [45]

allomorph The version of a **morpheme** as actually realized in speech or writing, e.g. *-s*, *-es*, and *-en* are all allomorphs (in writing) of the plural morpheme. [47]

allophone The version of **phoneme** as actually realized phonetically in speech. [42]

antonymy The **sense relation** of various kinds of opposing meaning between lexical items, e.g. 'big'/'small' (gradable); 'alive'/ 'dead' (ungradable). [57]

applied linguistics An area of enquiry which seeks to establish the relevance of theoretical studies of language to everyday problems in which language is implicated. [75]

arbitrariness The absence of similarity between the form of a linguistic sign and what it relates to in reality, e.g. the word 'dog' does not look like a dog. *See also* **design features**. [5]

bound morpheme An element of meaning which is structurally dependent on the word it is added to, e.g. the plural morpheme in 'dog^s': cf. **free morpheme**. *See also* **morpheme**. [45]

cohesion The ties that connect up units of language to form a **text**. [67]

collocation The co-occurence of **lexical items** in **text**, e.g. 'pious' regularly collocates with 'hope', and 'unforeseen' with 'circumstances'. *See also* **formulaic phrase**. [60]

communicative competence As defined by Hymes (*see* Text 12), the knowledge and ability involved in putting language to communicative use. *See also* **competence**. [28]

competence As defined by Chomsky (*see* Text 10), knowledge of the grammar of a language as a formal abstraction and distinct from the behaviour of actual use, i.e. **performance**: cf. *langue*. [24]

componential analysis The decomposition of lexical items into their basic elements of meaning, i.e. their **semantic components**. *See also* **denotation**. [57]

constituent A unit of grammatical structure, e.g. the sentence 'The lights went out' consists, at one level, of two constituents, the noun phrase ('the lights') and the verb phrase ('went out'). [34]

context Those aspects of the circumstances of actual language use which are taken as relevant to meaning. [38]

contrastive analysis The analysis of the significant differences between two (or more) languages. [76]

converseness The **sense relation** between two lexical items in which one of them implies the other, e.g. 'buy'/'sell'; 'give'/'take'. (If X buys a car from Y, this necessarily implies that Y sells a car to X.) [58]

cooperative principle A principle proposed by the philosopher Paul Grice whereby those involved in communication assume that both parties will normally seek to cooperate with each other to establish agreed meaning. [66]

corpus linguistics Linguistic description based on the extensive accumulation of actually occurring language data and its analysis by computer. [73]

critical discourse analysis The analysis of language use directed at, and committed to, discovering its concealed ideological bias. *See also* **discourse analysis**. [77]

denotation Aspects of reality encoded as **semantic components** in linguistic form. [56]

derivation That part of **morphology** concerned with the formation of **lexical items**. [46]

descriptive linguistics An enterprise whose priority is the description of particular languages rather than the devising of **theoretical models** for language in general. [75]

design features Those features of human language, like **arbitrariness** and **duality**, which are thought to distinguish it from other kinds of animal communication. [5]

diachronic Concerned with the process of language development over time: cf. **synchronic**. [22]

discourse analysis The analysis of language use in reference to the social conventions which influence communication. *See* **genre**. [76]

discourse The use of language in speech and writing to achieve **pragmatic** meaning: cf. **text**. [38]

duality The way meaningless elements of language at one level (sounds and letters) combine to form meaningful units (words) at another level. *See also* **design features**. [6]

error analysis The analysis and diagnosis of the errors of language learners. [76]

forensic linguistics The examination of linguistic evidence for legal purposes. [77]

formal linguistics The study of the abstract forms of language and their internal relations: cf. **functional linguistics**. [72]

formalist Concerned with linguistic forms in dissociation from their communicative function: cf. **functionalist**. [25]

formulaic phrase A (relatively) **fixed collocation**, e.g. 'no sooner said than done'; 'time is of the essence'. [60]

free morpheme An element of meaning which takes the form of an independent word: cf. **bound morpheme**. *See also* **morpheme**. [45]

functional linguistics The study of the forms of language in reference to their social function in communication: cf. **formal linguistics**. [71]

functionalist Concerned with the communicative functioning of linguistic forms: cf. **formalist**. [70]

genre A type of discourse in written or spoken **mode** with particular characteristics established by convention, e.g. a cooking recipe, a letter of application, a sermon. [67]

grammar The way linguistic forms combine as **morphemes** in the structure of words (*see* **morphology**) and as **constituents** in the structure of sentences (*see* **syntax**). [48]

grapheme The abstract form in written language, the underlying letter which is realized in various graphetic shapes in actual writing: cf. **phoneme/ phonetic**. [42]

graphological Concerned with the writing system and the principles of spelling, analagous to **phonological**. [35]

hyponymy The **sense relation** between terms in a hierarchy, where a more particular term (the hyponym) is included in the more general one (the **superordinate**): X is a Y, e.g. a beech is a tree, a tree is a plant. [59]

ideational function As defined by Halliday (*see* Text 6), the use of language as a means of giving structure to our experience of the third person world: cf. **interpersonal function**. [14]

illocution/illocutionary act That part of the **speech act** which involves doing and not just saying something, i.e. the performance of a recognized act of communication, e.g. promise, confession, invitation. [62]

illocutionary force The communicative value assigned to an **utterance** as the performance of an **illocutionary act**. An utterance is said to *be* a certain **illocution** because it *has* a certain force. [63]

inflection The **morphological** process which adjusts words by grammatical modification, e.g. in 'The rains came', 'rain' is inflected for plurality and 'came' for past tense. [46]

interlanguage The interim state of a second language learner's language. *See also* **Second Language Acquisition**. [76]

interpersonal function As defined by Halliday (*see* Text 6), the use of language for maintaining social roles and interacting with second-person others: cf. **ideational function**. [14]

intonation The variation in **pitch** and **stress** which gives beat and rhythm to the tune the voice plays in ordinary speech. [44]

Language Acquisition Device (LAD) According to Chomsky, the innate mental mechanism designed uniquely for the acquisition of language. [12]

langue Saussure's term (*see* Text 9) for the abstract linguistic system which is common social knowledge and which underlies individual uses of language, or **parole**: cf. **competence**. [21]

lexeme/lexical item A separate unit of meaning, usually in the form of a word (e.g. 'dog'), but also as a group of words (e.g. 'dog in the manger'). [29, 35]

medium The means whereby language is given physical expression in sounds and letters: cf. **mode**. [8]

mode The exploitation of a **medium** to achieve different kinds of communication, e.g. a speech is a mode of using the medium of speech. [8]

model An idealized abstraction of reality which represents its relevant features. [18]

morpheme An abstract element of meaning, which may be **free** in that it takes the form of an independent word, or **bound** in that it is incorporated into a word as a dependent part. [45]

morphology The study of the structure of words; of how **morphemes** operate in the processes of **derivation** and **inflection**. [36, 45]

paradigmatic Concerning the 'vertical' relationship of equivalence that holds between forms because they can replace each other in the same structure and so can be considered as different members of the same class, e.g. in the structure '_ plane landed' either 'the' or 'a' can occur, but not both, and so they are paradigmatically related: cf. **syntagmatic**. [33]

paralinguistic Concerning expressions of meaning which are part of communication but not part of language as such, e.g. gesture, grimace, and 'tone of voice'. [65]

parameter A general variable of **Universal Grammar** which is given particular values or 'settings' in different languages. [13]

parole Saussure's term (*see* Text 9) for the actual behaviour of individual language users, as distinct from the abstract language system, or **langue**: cf. **performance**. [21]

performance Chomsky's term for actual language behaviour as distinct from the knowledge that underlies it, or **competence**: cf. **parole**. [24]

perlocutionary effect That part of the **speech act** which has to do with the effect that it has on the receiver, e.g. an utterance with the **illocutionary force** of promise could, as **perlocutionary effect**, persuade, mislead, console, etc.: cf. **illocutionary force**. [63]

phoneme The abstract element of sound, identified as being distinctive in a particular language: cf. **morpheme**. [41]

phonemic Concerning phonemes and how they figure in the underlying sound system of languages. *See also* **phoneme**. [31]

phonetic Concerning the actual pronunciation of speech sounds and the various **allophonic** versions of **phonemes**. [31]

phonetics The description of sounds of speech as physical phenomena, how they are produced, and how they are received. In reference to the area of study, the term sometimes includes, sometimes excludes, **phonology**. [42]

phonological Concerned with **phonology**. **Phonological** features include **suprasegmental** phenomena as well as the **phonemic** features of individual sounds. [35]

phonology The study of the abstract systems underlying the sounds of language. [42]

pitch Voice level produced by varying tension in the vocal cords. [44]

pragmatics The study of what people mean by language when they use it in the normal **context** of social life: cf. **semantics**. [38, 61]

prefix An **affix** which is attached to the beginning of a word, e.g. *pre*^view, *un*^tie. [46]

proposition What is talked about in an utterance. That part of the **speech act** which has to do with **reference**. [62]

prototype What members of a particular community think of as the most typical instance of a lexical category, e.g. for some English speakers 'cabbage' (rather than, say, 'carrot') might be the prototypical vegetable. [74]

psycholinguistics The study of language and mind: the mental structures and processes which are involved in the acquisition and use of language: cf. **sociolinguistics**. [70]

reference The use of language to express a **proposition**, i.e. to talk about things in **context**. [62]

schema A mental construct of reality as culturally ordered and socially sanctioned: what people in a particular community regard as normal and predictable ways of organizing the world and communicating with others. [63]

Second Language Acquisition (SLA) The study of **interlanguage** and the factors which influence its emergence. [76]

semantic component Elements of meaning which combine in different ways to make up the **denotation** of different **lexical items**. [55]

semantics The study of meaning as encoded in language. This includes **denotation** and **sense relations**: cf. **pragmatics**. [27]

sense relations The relations which **lexical items** contract with each other within the language, e.g. 'cabbage' is a hyponym of the superordinate 'vegetable'; 'buy' and 'sell' are related as **converse** terms: cf. **denotation**. [57]

setting The particular fixing in a language of a **universal parameter** of language in general. [13]

sociolinguistics The study of language and society: how social factors influence the structure and use of language: cf. **psycholinguistics**. [70]

species-specific A term used by Chomsky to refer to language as a genetic endowment unique to the human species. [8]

speech act An act of communication performed by the use of language, either in speech or writing, involving **reference**, **force**, and **effect**. [63]

stress The prominence given to certain sounds in speech. [43]

stylistics The study of how literary effects can be related to linguistic features. [77]

suffix An **affix** which is attached to the end of words, e.g. 'cook^*er*', 'like^*ness*'. [46]

superordinate The term used to refer to the **sense relation** of inclusion. 'Vegetable', for example, is the superordinate within which 'cabbage' and 'carrot' are 'included' as **hyponyms**. [59]

suprasegmental Concerning features of spoken language, like **intonation**, other than separate sound segments. [44]

syllable Unit of sound consisting of a vowel (with or without consonants) which works like a pulse in the stream of speech. [43]

synchronic Concerned with the state of a language at any one time: cf. **diachronic**. [22]

synonymy The **sense relation** of equivalence of meaning between **lexical items**, e.g. 'small'/'little'; 'dead'/'deceased'. [58]

syntagmatic Concerning the 'horizontal' relationship of combination which holds between linguistic forms. They co-exist as different constituents in the same structure, each combining with the other, e.g. in 'The plane landed', 'The' combines with 'plane' combines with 'landed': cf. **paradigmatic**. [38]

syntax The **constituent** structure of sentences. [27, 37, 48]

text The product of the process of **discourse**. In written language, the text is produced by one of the parties involved (the writer) and is a part of the communication. In spoken language, the text will only survive the discourse if it is specially recorded. [38]

token A particular example of a general **type**. [29]

turn-taking The exchange of speaker role in verbal interaction. [67]

type An abstract, general category of things. [29]

Universal Grammar (UG)/Universal Parameters General abstract properties, or **parameters** of language as a whole which are claimed to be universal and innate. [12]

utterance An instance of language behaviour (in speech or writing), i.e. of *parole* or **performance**. It can be considered either as an act of speech, the physical manifestation of the **medium**, and the concern of **phonetics**, or as a **mode** of use in the **performance** of a **speech act**, and therefore the concern of **pragmatics**. [41]

Acknowledgements

The author and publisher are grateful to the following for permission to reproduce extracts from copyright material:

Ablex Publishing Corporation for an extract from W. Labov: 'The judicial testing of linguistic theory' in Deborah Tannen (ed.): *Linguistics in Context: Connecting Observation and Understanding*. Advances in Discourse Processes, Volume XXIV (Ablex 1988).

Blackwell Publishers for extracts from Diane Blakemore: *Understanding Utterances: An Introduction to Pragmatics* (1992); Noam Chomsky: *Rules and Representations* (1980); Deborah Schiffrin: *Approaches to Discourse* (1994); N.V. Smith: *The Twitter Machine* (1989); Ronald Wardhaugh: *Investigating Language: Central Problems in Linguistics* (1993).

Cambridge University Press and the authors for extracts from John Lyons: *Language and Linguistics: An Introduction* (1981), and *Introduction to Theoretical Linguistics* (1968); P.H. Matthews: *Morphology* (2nd edn.) (1991); J. R. Searle: *Speech Acts* (1969).

Faber & Faber Ltd. for 'August 1968' by W. H. Auden from *Collected Poems* edited by W. H. Mendelson.

HarperCollins Publishers for an extract from Noam Chomsky: *Reflections on Language* (Fontana).

Hodder Headline plc for an extract from M. A. K. Halliday: *Language as Social Semiotic* (Edward Arnold 1978).

Holt, Rinehart & Winston, Inc. for an extract from Victoria A.

Fromkin and Robert Rodman: *An Introduction to Language* (5th edn.) copyright © 1993 by Holt, Rinehart & Winston Inc.

International Thomson Publishing Services Ltd. for an extract from Martin Atkinson, David Kilby, and Iggy Roca: *Foundations of General Linguistics* (2nd edn.) (Unwin Hyman 1988).

Longman Group Ltd. for an extract from R.H. Robins: *General Linguistics: An Introductory Survey* (1989).

MIT Press for extracts from Noam Chomsky: *Aspects of the Theory of Syntax* (1965); B.L. Whorf: *Language, Thought and Reality* (1956).

Oxford University Press for an extract from John Sinclair: *Corpus, Concordance, Collocation* (1991).

Penguin Books Ltd. for extracts from David Crystal: *Linguistics* (Penguin Books 1971, rev. edn. 1981), copyright ® David Crystal, 1971; M.A.K. Halliday: 'Language structure and language function' in John Lyons (ed.): *New Horizons in Linguistics: An Introduction* (Penguin Books 1970, 1987), copyright ® John Lyons, 1970; Frank Palmer: *Grammar* (Penguin Books 1971, 2nd edn. 1984), copyright ® Frank Palmer 1971, 1983.

Random House Inc. for 'The Ogre' (retitled 'August 1968') by W.H. Auden reprinted from *W. H. Auden: Collected Poems* edited by W.H. Mendelson, copyright ® 1940, renewed 1968 by W.H. Auden; and for an extract from Noam Chomsky: *Reflections on Language* (Pantheon Books 1975), copyright © 1975 by J. Leonard Schatz, Trustee of the Chomsky Children's Trust # 2.

Routledge for an extract from Roy Harris: 'Redefining Linguistics' in Hayley G. Davis and Talbot J. Taylor (eds.): *Redefining Linguistics* (Routledge 1990).

Despite every effort to trace and contact copyright holders before publication, this has not always been possible. If notified, the publisher will be pleased to rectify any errors or omissions at the earliest opportunity.